*Tom O'Connor's Book of Liverpool Humour*

# TOM O'CONNOR'S book of Liverpool humour

Tom O'Connor
*with Graham Nown*

*Love to Shirley + Peter*

*Tom O'Connor*

Constable · London

First published in Great Britain 1987
by Constable and Company Limited
10 Orange Street, London WC2H 7EG
Copyright © 1987 Tom O'Connor and Graham Nown
Reprinted 1987
Set in Linotron Sabon 12pt by
Rowland Phototypesetting Limited
Bury St Edmunds, Suffolk
Printed in Great Britain by
St Edmundsbury Press Limited
Bury St Edmunds, Suffolk

British Library CIP data
O'Connor, Tom
    Tom O'Connor's book of Liverpool humour.
    I. Title   II. Nown, Graham
    828'.91407   PR6065.C5/

ISBN 0 09 468120 1

Picture Credits:
Paul Yaffe; *Liverpool Daily Post and Echo*; Stephen Porritt; Pontifica Fotografia; D. C. Thompson; Chris Capstick; T. H. Everitt; Tom O'Connor; David Owen; Ivan Gould.

Thanks to Robbins Music for permission to quote from 'Back Buchanan Street' by Gordon and Henry Dison.

To Theresa, my mum,
who would have been proud of this book

*At home in our Bootle backyard – before the wall was whitewashed.*

FFICIAL FAN CLUB:
S. GLORIA McCLURG
B ABBOTS CLOSE
ARE, GLASTONBURY
OMERSET BA6 9TF

# Contents

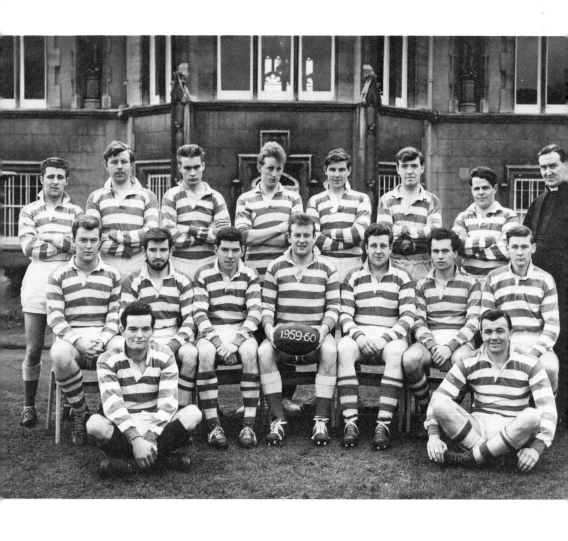

*The college rugby team – I'm third from the left in the middle row.*

# 1 *The Pool of Life*

Liverpudlians, they say, talk down their noses because their mouths have worn out.

What is certainly true is that it is almost as difficult to shut up a Scouser as it is to impress him. There is nowhere on earth greater than his native city. The more desolate or depressed it has become at times in recent history, the more unquenchable his pride in the place. The Scouser is always ready to leap to the defence of his birthplace: 'So Liverpool's fallin' down. Have you never been to Venice? Now, there's a dump . . .'

Across the city there is a strong feeling of 'if we haven't got it, then it's not worth having': 'The Taj Mahal? I'd rather have our shed.'

This peculiar flag-waving was best illustrated at the end of World War II, when Americans were pouring into the Port in their thousands. Liverpool had been devastated by the Blitz and, in the rubble of the waterfront, the Mayor addressed a mass meeting of dockers about the new visitors. As Liverpool's leading citizen he was concerned with international relations. The dockers were his ambassadors, and he was hoping for a show of diplomacy.

'Look lads,' he told them. 'Tomorrow there'll be boatloads of Yanks tying up here. You know what they're like. They'll be telling you how much bigger America is than Liverpool. Now humour them . . .'

Liverpool humour is sharper – and vastly different – to anything heard on the Lower East Side of New York, or the East End of London. It evolves from the Liverpudlian character and outlook on life, which very few people understand. A Scouser is witty but wary, rebellious but at the same time immensely logical. If something makes sense, he'll do it, particularly if there is the prospect of a fiddle. Otherwise, no force known to man can persuade him to pick up that spanner or shovel.

This was brought home to me when I worked on Canada Dock before going to college in Twickenham. I was employed by the Liverpool Warehousing Company to unload sacks of cocoa beans from the ships, weigh them, and put them onto lorries. Everyone was chasing a bonus, but two obstacles stood in the way.

The first was the fact that the sacks had to stand for two days to let the moisture drain out of them. The second was the docker, with the flat cap and Woody hanging from his mouth, who had to record the weights and add them up. Here was a man with a clipboard, the stub of an indelible pencil and purple marks all over his tongue. He was so slow struggling with columns of figures that none of us stood the slightest chance of making any money.

This was shortly before I specialized in teaching maths, and I noticed that most of the sacks tipped the scales at either just above or below a hundredweight.

'Instead of adding up all those columns,' I suggested, 'Why don't you use a hypothetical mean?'

The docker gave me a look as though I were trying to steal his ale and said: 'Yer wha?'

'Most of these sacks are coming off at around 115lbs or 110lbs. Pick a figure in the middle, say 112lbs, and just put down plus three, or minus two. It's quicker to add up and we'll get the job moving.'

The appeal lay in the logic. He thought about it, then pushed his clipboard and pencil at me.

'Okay,' he said. 'You do it.'

By the end of the week I had earned a bonus of £19.7s.6d which, in 1958, was equivalent to a pools win. The lads were euphoric. We were moving sacks so fast that they were coming straight off the ship, onto the scales and into the wagon without touching the ground. What we had all overlooked was the fact that the moisture was still in them. Three weeks later it had evaporated, and there was a call from the warehouse.

'According to my reckoning,' said the foreman on the other end of the line, 'there's three and a half tons of cocoa beans missing.'

When I told the docker with the purple tongue, he scratched his head and asked: 'What are we going to do about it?'

I pushed the clipboard and pencil back at him and said: 'Here you are, pal – you sort it out.'

And I legged it out of the dock gates as fast as I could.

The system worked because it made sense, but if the

dockers had been ordered to do it, no one would have agreed. There is a rebellious streak built into the Liverpudlian character which resists pressure from any direction. Some wrongly see it as cynicism, but it is really a case of the Scouser preferring to form his own opinions, unharassed.

I discovered this in my early days in the clubs, when I was still holding down the day job teaching. At the time, it was the pinnacle of every artist's ambition to play a converted cinema called the Wookey Hollow – a classy club, with chicken in the basket and Guinness in the fire extinguishers.

The floor, which still sloped from the days when it was the Lido Picture House, gave endless problems to waitresses staggering under trays of twenty-seven pints of bitter. From the stage it had the advantage that, when the audience was in an ugly mood, you could see them coming at you.

The comedian who appeared before me was very well known and was given a tremendous build-up. He bounced on to a deafening silence and went down like the *Lusitania*. The audience were taking no prisoners, and he was lucky to get away intact.

My instinct, as a young schoolmaster, was to call the whole thing off. If a great comic had had such a bad reception, my chances were absolutely nil. I confided in the compere, a man who knew his customers well, and told him I was thinking of going home.

'Don't worry, lad,' he said. 'Leave it to me. You'll go down a bomb.'

With that, he picked up the microphone and announced: 'We've a local kid next. A comic. He's no bloody good at all, but we've decided to cut our losses and put him on . . . Tom O'Connor.'

It was a shrewd move. The natural reaction of Liverpudlians to this was: 'Now hold on, pal – we'll be the judge of how good he is.' And I walked on to thunderous applause. By doing nothing more than giving the other comedian a big build-up, the compere had rubbed them up the wrong way and ruined the man before he even had a chance to start.

This streak of rebellion is not confined to any particular age group. A foreman at Ford's told me about an old man, in his sixties, who had been offered a part-time job sweeping the floor on the production line, where spot-welding was carried out.

'Here you are, grandad,' the foreman said on his first day. 'Here's your brush, and here's your goggles.'

'What's the goggles for?' the old man asked suspiciously.

'They're to protect you from the sparks.'

'Listen, son,' said Grandad. 'You might as well know now. There'll be no sparks coming from this brush.'

The gift of the quick answer is often used to put outsiders firmly in their place. It is also a handy defence against anything beyond the Scouser's field of experience.

I once watched an amiable American visitor in the Sixties studying a gang of council labourers laying a pavement in Scotland Road. He seemed interested in the way they went about it, and asked: 'What do you call this kind of work in England?'

'Flaggin',' one of them told him and, like every Liverpudlian, could not resist going into a long routine about how the job was done: 'Now, you lay your sand . . . then you drop your flag in . . . you knock it with the rubber hammer . . .'

Towards the end of this verbal instruction manual, the workman asked: 'Is this what you do – back in the States – flaggin'?'

'No, no,' the American smiled. 'I'm in micro-engineering. We have to work to a thousandth of an inch.'

'Oh, that's no use to us, pal,' said the flagger. 'In this job you have to be spot on.'

Some people, of course, interpret the fast answer-back as aggression. True, Liverpool does have a bit of a reputation in that direction. It has always been a violent city, but in the most idiosyncratic way. Where else, for instance, could you walk into a pub on 25 December and hear someone say: 'Don't hit him – it's Christmas.'? On Boxing Day, of course, anything can happen.

While Liverpudlians think like chess players, slowly working out the implications of every move, speed and surprise remain the source of Scouse wit. A floor-them-with-the-first-punch philosophy. Those who fire fastest from the mouth naturally work closely with the public. The only way for one Scouser to put another in his place is to make sure he doesn't get up again. Bus conductors, butchers and especially waitresses are experts in the technique:

'Hey love, there's a fly in me cake.'

'Give it back, I'll give you a currant.'

Those Americans who invaded Liverpool in the aftermath of World War II had their first taste of the dry reply in the Dock Road cafés. Anyone foolish enough to cross forks with a waitress on her home ground knew he had met his match. She can still be found today – the arche-

*Bootle's answer to Geoff Boycott.*

typal Fag Ash Lil, armed with a damp cloth and her hair done up like a four-pound loaf.

There is one now legendary story about an American serviceman who celebrated the end of a week on ship's rations by ordering the biggest meal on the menu in a Dock Road café.

'I'll have the sheep's head,' he told the waitress, who was waiting to have the Woodbine removed from her mouth by surgery.

'One sheep's head . . .' she called to the kitchen.

When it arrived, he complained: 'Hey, I don't want it cooked like this. I want it done American style.'

Fag Ash Lil was unmoved.

'Take the brains out . . .' she called to the kitchen.

Tony Christie, the singer, found himself in a Dock Road café in the early hours of the morning after a late show. He ordered a full breakfast of bacon, egg and sausages, and tucked in ravenously. When Tony put the fork into his egg, he was amazed to see the yolk disappear completely from his plate. It was a total mystery until he lifted up the plate and found that it had a hole in the centre, about the size of a pea. The café had obviously bought a job lot of cake stands, and unscrewed the base from each plate.

'Excuse me,' he said to the waitress, 'there's a hole in my plate.'

'They're all like that,' she said. 'I hang them on a nail to dry when I've washed them.'

Tony was quite puzzled by this.

'But what would you have done,' he asked, 'if I'd ordered soup?'

The waitress gave him a look as though he were remedial and said: 'Lent you me chewy, of course.'

I think this proof enough of the old verse:

You can always tell a French girl,
You can always tell a Swiss.
You can tell a girl from Sweden
By the way she's learned to kiss.
You can tell a señorita,
You can tell a girl who's Dutch;
You can also tell a Liverpool girl
– But you can't tell her much.


It must be significant that there was such an interest in chess in Liverpool as early as 1813 that the *Liverpool Mercury* launched the world's first newspaper chess column. Somehow the interest never completely disappeared. Liverpool logic still resembles a chess player's, and comes into operation when a proposal of any kind is involved. A Scouser can evaluate the odds faster than Ladbroke's computer, and work out if anyone is trying to take advantage of him.

Barry Mason the songwriter, told me that he was driving along Lime Street at the time *Delilah* was a world-wide hit. Barry pulled up at some traffic lights and, outside the car window, heard a Scouser whistling the number he had written. He was leaning on the pole of the traffic lights, eating chips from a paper bag.

Barry, who was overcome with delight at hearing someone in the street whistling one of his compositions, wound down the window.

'I happened to write that,' he said with a warm smile. 'I'm Barry Mason.'

The Scouser stopped whistling and stared at him, a chip poised half-way to his mouth.

Write what?'

'*Delilah*. I wrote it.'

'No you didn't,' said the Scouser, and carried on eating his chips.

Barry was rather fazed by this.

'I'm sorry, but I did,' he insisted.

'I've got the record at home,' the bloke said. 'Les Reed wrote it.'

'That's right,' said Barry, brightening. 'Les wrote the tune, I wrote the words . . .'

'I wasn't whistling the words,' said the Scouser, and continued with his chips.

This deep-rooted suspicion always reminds me of my Uncle Harry, who spent most of his working life as a conductor on the Corporation buses. One of the many family tales about him concerned two nuns, riding on the top deck up Brownlow Hill to the Cathedral. It was one of those hot days when the bus was overcrowded, Uncle Harry was sweating bullets and his bag of fiddle was getting heavier by the hour.

'Okay, girls,' he said. 'Fares, please.'

'I'm afraid,' one of the nuns said, 'that we've left our purse behind at the convent.'

'All right,' said Harry, pulling out his notebook, 'Names . . .'

The nuns told him who they were and added, by way of explanation: 'We're the Sisters of St John the Baptist from Bootle.'

Harry went downstairs satisfied, but two stops later he was bounding back up, looking murderous.

'Right, you two,' he ordered. 'Off'.

The nuns looked alarmed, but Uncle Harry wasn't taken in.

'On yer way,' he told them. 'John the Baptist's dead.'

# 2  *Parliamo Scouse*

The Liverpudlian character is unique, but plumbing the depths of the language can pose problems to outsiders. Weekend crash courses are available at the Wine Lodge, where the emphasis is on 'crash'. Lesson One is learning to duck without spilling your glass of white.

What Liverpudlians may lack in grammar, they make up for with a sound grasp of the alphabet, a fact I witnessed at a strike meeting when I worked on the North End docks. The steward had been locked in pay talks with the management and came back looking depressed to report to the men. The dockers gathered round as he clambered onto a crate.

'Lads,' he said, 'they won't budge on the money. I've asked for it, I've begged for it, I've even cried for it . . .'

'Have you tried working for it?' one of them shouted from the back of the crowd.

'Hey, give us a chance,' the steward said. 'I'm workin' me way up. I haven't come to W yet.'

Part of the language problem lies in pronunciation. We tend to sound our Ts like Ss, so that listening to a crowd of girls conversing in a pub can sound like a dozen bottles of stout being opened simultaneously. Even Scousers are embarrassed by it.

When a bloke escorts his girl safely to the front door after a night out, he is usually three-quarters of a block down the street when she starts: 'Goodnice . . . That wuz grace . . . Reely grace . . .'

'Hello,' he thinks, 'she's showin' me up . . .'

And he puts down his head and quickens his pace before the whole street wakes up.

An interesting point here is that, to the outside world, a Scouser seldom shows embarrassment. The scene: a flight to a holiday resort anywhere in Europe. Jimmy Mack, from Fazackerly, and his wife are on their first trip abroad. As soon as the drinks trolley has been round, the mouth organ comes out. Without a care in the world, Jimmy, with his missus on the spoons, belts out half a dozen choruses of 'Mule Train'. Jimmy can't understand why no one wants to join in – they always do on a chara. The silence is total. At this point, only a man from Liverpool can turn round to face two hundred pairs of hostile eyes and say accusingly: 'All right, nose. You've all had a good look, have you?'

Foreigners, in particular, experience a total communications problem. Those early G.I.'s might as well have been talking to Ukranians when they met Liverpool dockers:

'Have you got a light Mac?'

'Er, no – a dark overcoat.'

Despite being a cosmopolitan city, there is not always a warm welcome for strangers. A Hamburg sailor, with little grasp of English, and even less Scouse, came off his ship. After asking several dockers the way to the city centre, one of them offered to help.

He scribbled on a scrap of paper and explained slowly: 'Here. If you get lost, hand this to somebody. You'll soon get sorted out.'

Half a mile on, the German stopped a policeman and handed him the note.

'Please,' he said. 'A man wrote this down. He said I must show if lost.'

The policeman unfolded the piece of paper, then handed it back to the sailor. It read: 'Tell him nothin'.'

Liverpudlians can be almost poetic in their gift for description. Small wonder Lennon and McCartney wrote such beautiful, succinct lyrics after growing up in a city with so much talent everywhere. Ordinary people in the street have a directness which paints an instant picture.

'She's got teeth like the Ten Commandments,' one woman remarked. 'All broken.'

On the Kop, well known for its witticisms, a disgusted Liverpool fan turned to his neighbour when a player lost the ball and said: 'I've seen milk turn quicker.'

Scousers are well known for their spontaneous remarks about physical features. 'A face like a blind cobbler's thumb', or 'a face like a busted wellie', are common. 'Teeth queuing up to get to the front' is another, along with 'a face even his mother couldn't love', or 'When she sucks a lemon, the lemon pulls a face'.

One of my favourites is the archetypal woman with her hair permanently in rollers: 'She had a head like a bucket of chips.'

After a hard night on the ale, when the brain sends a message to one eye to open up and take a look at what's going on, Scousers have their own term for a hangover. 'Me head', we say, 'was goin' like a box of frogs.'

And the toddler outside church in her best Sunday dress: 'She was walkin' round like a pigeon in a frock.'

They are delivered with a speed that a playwright or poet in the South might never emulate.

I heard two blokes discussing a friend's misfortune:

FIRST MAN: 'Unlucky? He'd break his leg in the Eye Hospital.'

SECOND MAN: 'Aye. If it was raining soup he'd be standing with a fork in his hand.'

When I was young I was keen on sport, but had the disadvantage of being extremely thin. The first time I jumped into the swimming baths the instructor called: 'Who threw those braces in the water?'

One of my great interests was athletics, despite once overhearing a teacher say: 'He couldn't win a race – the tape would cut his neck . . .'

I can't help feeling sorry for all those Frenchmen and Germans who spend a lifetime learning English, only to visit Liverpool and find that we don't speak it. Somewhere, there must be a touch of Irish in the language, because Scousers have a gift for what I can only describe as nonsensical sense. They use phrases which sound reasonable only to other Scousers. It is quite common, for instance, to hear two men on a street corner arranging to have a pint.

'I'll see you in the Blue House, then,' one says.

'No one goes there now,' the other replies, 'It's always full.'

Once in the bar, one of them will probably say to the other: 'Don't turn round, but look who's behind you.'

This is roughly equivalent to the person who approaches the empty bar stool next to you, and asks: 'Is anybody sitting there?'

And you stare very carefully at it before replying: 'I don't think so . . .'

There is a nice touch of whimsy about Scouse. One of my grandmother's favourite expressions was: 'It's not like the old days, when you could make a meal out of nothing if you had the stuff.'

After a hard day washing and cleaning no one was alarmed when she said: 'I'm so tired, I could go upstairs and throw meself down.'

Compare this with the mother who takes her son to the doctor and asks: 'Can you do something with his face? He's had it a while and it's spreading.'

Or the commonly encountered: 'I had to go to the vet – the cat's been as sick as a dog.'

Liverpool vets, incidentally, have not always had a polished bedside manner. About twenty years ago a TV documentary called *Morning in the Streets* took a look at a day in the life of a Liverpool terrace. Two women were discussing a visit to the vet had just made.

'He picked our budgie up off the floor of the cage, took one look at him and said: "He's dead. That'll be 7s.6d. for the visit." Then he threw it straight on the back of the fire and said: "Plus another five bob for cremation . . ."'

Women are quite gifted in the art of nonsensical sense. I heard of two of them meeting on a bus, and one greeted the other with: 'Hello Mary, how's your new teeth?'

'Terrible,' her friend said. 'I'm leaving them out till I get used to them.'

Many Liverpool women spend their entire lives wrestling with the problems of medical terminology. The conversation above soon drifted into: 'How's your hubby?'

'He's in hospital,' Mary said. 'They're feeding him intravenously.'

'Funny, isn't it?' her friend sympathized, 'if you gave him that at home, he wouldn't eat it, would he?'

Later, there was this exchange: 'Does your leg still bother you, Mary?'

'Only when I stand on it. It's me various veins.'

This similar fragment came from a very indignant lady: '. . . so I gave it him straight. "Call yerself a chiropodist," I said, "yer couldn't stuff a parrot" . . .'

Years later, I'm still trying to figure that one out.

Liverpool's local radio airwaves hum with medical malapropisms. Towards the end of a phone-in on Radio Merseyside, a caller said to DJ Billy Butler: 'I've got to go now. Me mam's in hospital.'

'Sorry to hear that,' said Billy. 'Has she had an operation?'

'Yeah, they took everything out. A full hysterical rectomy.'

Phone-ins often have a habit of drifting unintentionally into medical topics. One minute they can be talking about anything, from politics to the price of petrol, then seconds later they're straight into illness again:

BILLY: 'Are you married, love?'

WOMAN: 'Yeah, but me hubby's not been too well. He's getting over a coronary trombonist. They thought it was a tuba on the brain at first, but it was non-militant . . .'

Once you develop an ear for it, nonsensical sense is suddenly everywhere. I recall a snatch of conversation I once overheard in a pub in Garston.'

'That's a good jacket,' one bloke said to another.

'Yeah, it's a donkey jacket. Really hard-wearing. They last you a lifetime. This is me fourth.'

As children we tended to obey instructions without question, which was perhaps a good thing when mothers, like mine, used to say: 'Run round to the corner shop for five pounds of spuds. And don't get any big ones – they're too heavy to carry.'

I once heard a friend of my mother in T. J. Hughes, a famous cut-price Liverpool department store, asking the salesgirl: 'Do you have any underpants for a man with a forty-inch chest?'

The assistant, a Scouser of course, produced a pair without a flicker.

Fathers are always hopeless at buying clothes. In the same department store, I caught one dad saying:

'I want a sweater for the lad.'

'What size is he?' the salesgirl asked.

'Dunno. He rides a bike with a sixteen-inch wheel.'

Small boys always came in for an earful of nonsensical sense when they climbed trees. Many's the time I've heard a mother shout: 'Don't come running to me when you break both your legs . . .'

Warnings were always dished out when kids went off to play: 'You stay out of that bombed house. The place is alive with dead rats. There's holes a foot high in that floor.'

Everyone in my neighbourhood had a back yard and, once in a while, it was given a fresh lick of whitewash. I remember Dad discussing the problem in some depth with the next-door neighbour:

'I'm thinking of having the yard whitewashed,' Dad said.

'What colour were you thinking of whitewashing it?' the neighbour asked.

*Helping the champ with some finishing touches.*

'I'm thinking of doing it green.'

'Look,' the neighbour said, weighing up the situation. 'My son'll do that for you. He'll whitewash it any colour you like. It won't cost you a penny, and it'll be a few bob for the boy, as well.'

It is possible to hear entire conversations like this which, on reflection, mean absolutely nothing – especially on the rare occasion when a Scouser is lost for words:

'Have you seen your mate – the big feller?'

'Who's that?'

'You know . . . He married Teresa thingy . . . They used to live up whatsit street . . . The old man used to have the – er – whatd'yacallit business . . .'

'What about him?'

'He's not been well, you know.'

'Hasn't he?'

'No. They took most of it away. Well, not all of it, of course. The doctor said it could have gone either way . . . Didn't you know?'

'Well, I did hear something, but not the details until now.'

My father Pat, a Cork man from Kinsale, has that blend of Liverpool-Irish wit which is often unconscious. I still smile at the thought of him, when he weighed twenty-three stone, lying on the sofa in his vest watching the Olympic pole vault finals on television. With a Capstan Full Strength in one hand and a pint of Guinness in the other, he said: 'This feller's hopeless. I could do better meself.'

The Irish have a gift of wit which I last came across when the Tom O'Connor Roadshow was in Londonderry. Slogans about the Anglo-Irish Agreement were daubed on all the buildings, and someone had painted on a wall in six-foot-high letters: ULSTER SAYS NO. Alongside it had been added: THE MAN FROM DEL MONTE SAYS YES. This was perhaps only matched by a sign painted across over a bridge over the M62 motorway, on the outskirts of Manchester, by Liverpool supporters: YOU ARE NOW ENTERING A TROPHY-FREE ZONE.

For sheer speed of delivery, I firmly believe that the man who can outdraw a Liverpudlian has not yet been born. Anyone who steps on a Liverpool bus will sample it before the journey is over. Uncle Harry, the conductor, was an expert:

'Do you stop at the Adelphi?' one passenger enquired.

'On my wages?' he asked.

He was always determined that no one would get away with underpaying while he was in charge of the bus. A woman with her son handed him some coppers and said: 'One and a half to the Pier Head.'

'You'll have to pay full fare for that kid. He's over fourteen,' Uncle Harry insisted.

'He can't be,' the woman replied. 'I've only been married twelve years.'

'I'm taking fares,' said Harry, 'not confessions.'

Working in Liverpool, of course, he often met his match.

'Spellow Lane,' he called, as a crowd of passengers were climbing aboard. 'Inside only . . .'

'Where's the top half going to?' one of them asked.

Scouse is definitely spreading. I believe it has something to do with all that Welsh water we drink, because the language has now filtered westward as far as Rhyl. Drive along the North Wales coast these days and it is quite common to hear: 'Yer know warr I mean, like, look-you, isn't it?'

The influence has been found even farther afield. When my dad's pal, Charlie Hargreaves, went to Paris he sat down to breakfast at a pavement café. As he picked up his knife and fork, a Frenchman eating at the next table said:

'Bon appetit.'

Charlie nodded and said: 'Charlie Hargreaves.'

'Bon appetit,' the man smiled again.

'Charlie Hargreaves,' Charlie replied.

The waiter was bemused by this.

'The gentleman is actually wishing you a good appetite, sir.'

'Oh, I didn't realize that,' Charlie apologized. 'Bon appetit, pal.'

'Charlie Hargreaves,' the Frenchman replied.

With that eternal Scouse talent for believing we know everything, my grandfather tried to learn French for his first trip abroad.

'It took me twenty minutes,' he announced, 'But I've cracked it. I read the book. There's nothing to it.'

'Are you really sure you're going to cope?' my father asked.

'No problem,' said Grandad. 'If I'm hungry I'll just go to a farmhouse and say: "Avez-vous un huff?" And they'll give me an egg.'

'What do you do if you want two eggs?' Dad asked.

'Easy,' Grandad said. 'You just say: "Avez-vous trez huff?" They give you three eggs, and you give them one back.'

This, I suppose, is the essence of Liverpool logic. A philosophy summed up in the immortal words of our local pub quiz league referee:

'Now then, Harry,' the team warned him. 'Don't give us any hard questions.'

'There's no such thing as a hard question,' he said. 'If you know the answers, they're all easy.'

*You can always tell a Liverpool girl — but you can't tell her much.*

Or, as someone once said to him at the bar as he downed his tenth pint of bitter:

'D'you know, Harry, I don't know how you can treat your body like that. You drink too much, you smoke too much, then there's all them chips and fry-ups you eat.'

'What can I do?' Harry shrugged. 'If I gave up everything and turned vegetarian, I'd end up dyin of nothin', wouldn't I?'

Liverpudlians are possessed of a blend of common sense and cocky optimism which, for me, was best illustrated by the story of the Scouse soldier sent on an Arctic survival course.

Like all Liverpudlians he could not keep his mouth shut, and the patience of the Canadian instructor began to wear thin:

'You Liverpool people think you know everything,' he snapped. 'But you know nothing. Without me, you'll die out here in the Yukon.'

As they strapped on their snowshoes, he warned: 'You can survive the cold, but the biggest danger out here is a hungry grizzly. That's the one thing a gun can't stop.'

Two days into the frozen tundra, there was a roar and they both turned to find a nine-foot beast bearing down on them.

'It's all over,' the instructor gasped. 'Say your prayers, Scouse. It's a hungry grizzly.'

The Liverpudlian ignored him, pulled out a pair of brand new Nike running shoes from his rucksack, and bent down to put them on.

'Forget it Scouse,' the instructor shouted in despair. 'You can't outrun a hungry grizzly.'

'No,' said Jimmy disappearing into the distance, his legs going like pistons, 'but I can outrun you.'

Scouse logic is simple and, on some occasions, can be

so uncomplicated that it clouds common sense. There is a true story, of someone I knew, who lost his wife. He came home from work one day to find that she had disappeared, without even leaving a note. He reported her to the police who promised to put her name on their missing persons list.

A week later the desk sergeant rang him and enquired:

'Has your wife come back yet?'

'No sign of her,' said the husband.

'I'm sorry to have to tell you, but I think there's some bad news . . . We think she's been found floating in the canal.'

'Well, that can't be her,' the husband said. 'She can't swim.'

# 3  *No Surrender*

Liverpool has two cathedrals, which face each other at opposite ends of appropriately-named Hope Street. One is the tall, sandstone Anglican cathedral, the other the modern tent-like Catholic cathedral, known affectionately as Paddy's Wigwam. Scousers support one or the other, as they do Liverpool or Everton.

I attended a Catholic school in Bootle and gained an early insight into the cloistered life of priests and nuns. Our school dances always went on later than permitted, and the band played so loud that the Reverend Mother in the convent next door had a restless night. After one dance which had gone completely over the top, she complained to the parish priest and demanded that he should do something about it.

The following morning, Sunday, he climbed into the

pulpit with a face like thunder and read the congregation the riot act:

'Youse all went too far at that school dance,' he roared. 'The Reverend Mother and I couldn't get a wink of sleep all night.'

He may have had his off days but, like all Catholic priests, was always available in times of need. Every parishioner knows that he can turn to a priest in the event of emergency, wherever he might be. One Liverpudlian safe in this reassuring knowledge, was seen walking down the aisle of the Lime Street to Euston express calling: 'Is there a Catholic priest aboard? For God's sake, is anyone here a Catholic priest?'

His situation seemed so desperate that a man sitting nearby rose to his feet and said: 'I'm a Rabbi, can I be of help?'

'I don't think so,' said the Scouser. 'I want to borrow a bottle-opener.'

Our local priest, who complained about the school dance, used to terrify us with his sermons. He would wave his arms and threaten everyone with hell and damnation if they stepped out of line. One Sunday he worked himself up to such a pitch, shouting and thumping the rail of the pulpit, that a little boy grabbed his mother's arm and said: 'If he breaks out of there, Mam, he'll kill us.'

When he called round on his parish visits, everyone had to have a wash and be on their best behaviour. Priests have this effect on Liverpool families. As soon as they set foot over the doorstep everyone tries to become well-mannered and refined – picking their noses with their little fingers, eating chips with gloves on and serving up the scouse with salad cream.

It is exactly like the old Liverpool story of the seven

kids being bundled off to bed as soon as the priest knocked at the door, in case they said something they shouldn't. They all slept in one bed under dad's old overcoat because they didn't have enough blankets. As the priest sat down to tea – dad had the shaving mug, and mum the one with the crack in it – terrible screams and thumps began to issue from the bedroom next door.

'Excuse me, Father,' the mother apologized and disappeared to quell the riot.

'Listen you lot,' she warned, 'one more squeak and you'll feel the back of me hand. You're showing us up in front of Father Murphy. Now what's the trouble?'

'We're freezing cold,' one of them complained. 'Our Jimmy keeps pinchin' all the overcoat for himself.'

'How many times do I have to tell you,' hissed the mother. 'It isn't an overcoat, it's a duvet. Now shut up.'

Five minutes later, as the priest was nibbling the custard creams, there were more crashes and cries from the bedroom.

'What's going on in there?' the mother shouted, losing control.

After a moment's silence, a small voice piped up: 'Mam, our Jimmy's ripped the sleeve off the duvet.'

Everyone jumped to it on such occasions.

'I hope everyone in this house is still going regularly to Mass,' a visiting priest said.

'Oh yes, Father,' the mother told him.

'And I take it you're still reading the Bible to the children?'

'I read the Bible to them every morning and every night, Father. Mary – go and get that big book I'm always reading . . .'

Little Mary disappeared and came back with the Littlewoods catalogue.

*Starting a sponsored walk in Southport – thank heavens for the law.*

Now priests may rule their parishes with a rod of iron, but they in turn are answerable to higher authorities. The clergy rely on the support of the church and know that, in times of doubt, they can turn for ecclesiastical advice to the Archbishop.

There is a story of one Scouse priest who faced such a dilemma when he opened up his church one morning and was confronted by a complete stranger, sitting cross-legged on the altar.

'Who are you?' the Father asked, taken aback.

'I am God,' the man answered.

'Just wait there a minute,' the priest said, and got straight on the telephone to the Archbishop's office.

'I need a bit of advice,' he whispered. 'There's a bloke here sitting on my altar, and he says he's God. What should I do?'

The Archbishop considered all the implications of this. 'We can't take any chances,' he said. 'Pick up a brush and look busy . . .'

It takes a brave man to tackle the church but, according to historical evidence, at least one Scouser has tried. The following invoice, dated 1896 and submitted by a local painter and decorator, was found in the loft of an Everton church:

For repainting Heaven, and doing one or two jobs on the Damned
For scrubbing down the Garden of Eden . . .£2.10/-
For tidying up Goliath and putting a new stone in David's sling
I am submitting this bill in all good faith, and the sincere hope that I have not done the work for charity.

The Scouse faithful have been known to make the long and ancient pilgrimage to Rome – providing there is a European Cup fixture on. To save money on the trip two of them decided to take a tent and camp out overnight.

In the early hours they found a quiet open space and pitched the tent. Next morning they awoke to find themselves in the middle of a crowd of thousands of pilgrims in St Peter's Square, waiting for the Pope to emerge on the Vatican balcony.

The Pontiff stepped out and made his familiar sign of the Cross to bless the crowd – one long vertical stroke, followed by a horizontal sweep of the white sleeve.

The Liverpudlians did not have a good vantage spot, and one of them asked his mate: 'Who's he wavin' at?'

'It must be us, Joey,' said his pal, straining his eyes. 'I think he's sayin', "Take that tent down, and get it out of here".'

Liverpool's real religion is, of course, football. Prayers are regularly made and candles lit to guide the fortunes of the Reds and Blues. God, Scousers firmly believe, is clearly not a supporter of struggling Tranmere.

One of my favourite stories is about the Liverpool team manager who wrote to the Pope asking him to bless the team at the start of the season. A few weeks later things were going so badly that he telephone the Vatican to find out what had gone wrong.

'We're losing game after game, Your Holiness. You've got to help us out . . .'

'Oh, I'm too old, my son,' the Pope demurred.

'I said *pray* for us, not *play* for us,' the manager pleaded.

Surprisingly, in a city so divided between the Orange and the Green, Scousers are happy to turn to religion of any colour in times of doubt:

'I've got this problem, Harry,' one bloke confided in his mate.

'What's that?'

'I'm going out with two girls and I don't know which one to marry.'

His pal was concerned.

'What religion are you?' he asked.

'I'm a Protestant, why?'

'Well, I'm a Catholic,' said Harry. 'And I think I can help you. Go into our church, kneel down, and the Lord will guide you.'

His friend was not convinced, but he went along with the advice. Two minutes later he was seen running out of church into the pub, ecstatic.

'The Lord's done it,' he shouted. 'I knelt down, and the answer was there, written right across the altar. It said 'ave Maria.'

This sense of religion is impressed in children from an early age. Even at infant school we were expected to know all the major Biblical characters, though naturally in Liverpool one or two unfamiliar ones crept in. I recall one Christmas when we all had to draw a Nativity scene and tell the story. The teacher studied the picture drawn by the lad who sat next to me and said: 'Tell us all who these people are, Tommy.'

'Well, Miss, there's Mary, an' baby Jesus, an' the big fat man.'

'You mean Joseph, I think . . .'

'No,' said Tommy. 'The big fat man.'

'Who's the big fat man?' teacher asked, puzzled.

'You know. He's always there with the other two – Round John Virgin, mother and child . . .'

Apart from its two major denominations, Liverpool has always been a major stopping place for touring

revivalist preachers. I remember times when Liverpool Stadium would be packed to capacity with crowds waiting for a miracle cure. Yates's Wine Lodge would put on a mobile bar, and attendance was almost as big as a Derby game.

To warm up the audience, a woman usually took the microphone and gave her testimony:

'Last night I was in the arms of Satan,' she would say. 'But tonight I'll be in the arms of the Lord.'

And a lone voice would call from the back: 'How are you fixed for tomorrow night?'

Half-way through the evening they passed round the collection boxes. I heard a story about a girl rattling one of them under the nose of an old Scouser:

'Can you spare a shilling for God?'

He looked at it suspiciously and asked her: 'How old are you?'

'Seventeen,' she said.

'I'm ninety-one,' the old feller told her. 'I'll see Him before you do. I'll pay Him meself.'

The star attraction of the evening was the preacher determined to heal someone:

'Friends,' he would shout, pacing the platform, 'I want anyone with an affliction in this stadium to come up here and stand on this stage.'

'Here ya, lad,' somebody called. 'Charlie'll come up. He's on crutches. Broke his leg.'

'Who'll come up with Charlie?' the preacher asked, encouraged.

'I'll come up with him,' called another voice. And an old man named Fred, with a cleft palate, made his way to the platform.

*There's only one way to treat an unruly audience.*

'Charlie,' the preacher intoned. 'I want you to go behind the screen on your crutches. I want you to raise your eyes to the Lord, and throw your right crutch into the audience . . .'

A moment later the crutch came flying out.

'Halleluja,' a thousand cried.

'Charlie,' the preacher ordered. 'I want you now to raise your eyes to the Lord and throw out your left crutch . . .'

Seconds later, the other crutch was tossed into the crowd.

'Halleluja,' the cry went up again.

'Right,' said the preacher, turning to Fred. 'Go behind the screen, friend. Raise your eyes to the Lord and speak the first words that come into your head . . .'

Fred disappeared behind the screen and the crowd waited for another miracle.

'Speak up, Fred,' called the preacher. 'Let's hear you.'

Fred shuffled out.

'Charlie's fell over . . .' he announced.

Of all the accusations levelled at Liverpool, it can never be said that Scousers have no heart. I remember the story of an eighty-year-old who was struggling to survive on his pension. Desperate for money, he decided to appeal to the Almighty.

The old boy took a pen and postcard and wrote:

Dear God,
    I'm stuck for a few bob. If I had £100 it would last me the rest of me life. Please send it as soon as you can.
    Yours faithfully,
    Harry

He then addressed it to 'God', c/o Heaven', stuck on a tuppence ha'penny stamp and shuffled to the letter box.

One of the postmen at the sorting office read it, and was touched. He organised a whip-round among his work-mates, and raised £95. The postman sealed it in an envelope, together with a note which read:

From God. Enclosed: your money.

And they posted it off to him.

When the old fellow received it, he sent a postcard back immediately:

Dear God,

I got the money you sent me. Unfortunately, there was only £95 in the envelope. It must have been one of them robbin' swines at the GPO.

# 4 A Few Scoops of Ale

Showbusiness, somebody once said, is a funny way to be a hero. Some of the artists who worked the clubs in my early years deserved medals; I still wonder why they punished themselves. I remember standing in the wings, waiting to go on after one particular novelty act. He had walked out in a loincloth and stuck needles through his cheeks. From where I was standing, I could see the blood quite clearly. Everyone was drinking and paying no attention to him.

He followed this up by chewing razor blades. Blood was this time pouring down his lips, and those in the audience who noticed it were muttering, 'Phoney'.

Then he butted bricks with his head until I could see the bumps visibly rising. His finale was to smash pint mugs all over the stage and lie down on them while twenty-stone drunks stood on his chest. When he rose to his feet to take a bow, jagged pieces of glass were hanging from his back.

To close the show he strolled on, immaculately dressed, with bruises all over his forehead, sticking plaster on his cheek and dried blood round his mouth, singing, ' . . . Oh, the good life . . .'

One of my enduring memories was being booked to play four clubs a night, and trying to find them in the dark. The streets were usually deserted and, as the only people around were drunk, asking directions was hopeless. On one occasion, with only ten minutes to spare before I was due on stage, I stopped a drunk to ask him the way to Higher Bebbington British Legion.

'I'm going up there, pal,' he offered. 'Give us a lift and I'll show you the way.'

He climbed unsteadily into the car, and said: 'Straight on, Jim.'

After that, he didn't speak another word. Six miles up the road I was glancing at my watch, feeling desperate.

'Do you really know where this club is?' I asked him.

'Yeah,' he finally answered. 'But it's rubbish there. We're going to a much better one than that . . .'

This kind of thing happens frequently. Just recently I was in the car with Tony, my roadie, who drives me when we are touring. It was in the early hours of the morning and – sure enough – the only sign of life was a drunk leaning in a doorway.

He was staring at a petrol stain in a puddle, wondering if he had found a dead rainbow, when I got out to ask him where the Hacienda Club was.

He thought for a while, then said: 'No. But I'll find out for you.'

And, with that, he lurched over to Tony, sitting in the

car at the kerbside, and asked him for directions. Two minutes later he walked back to me, as though it were uphill all the way, and said:

'This feller's looking for it, too. If you play your cards right, he might give you a lift.'

There is, of course, no cure for strong drink. I've often been tempted to change from Guinness to draught Windowlene. You still wake up the next day with a thumping head, but very clear eyes. The beer in some of the places I played was so flat that it should have been sold in envelopes, but blokes were still ten deep at the bar, knocking it back.

Listening to drunks makes you realize that, after a few scoops of ale, the Scouser's brain completely loses control of his mouth. The following conversation was overheard at the bar at Yates's Wine Lodge:

> DRUNK: 'You're my best pal, Jimmy, and I don't forget that.'
> JIMMY: 'Right.'
> DRUNK: 'If I won the pools, Jimmy, I'd give you half of it . . .'
> JIMMY: 'Right.'
> DRUNK: 'You know, if I had two mansions, Jim, I'd give you one of them . . .'
> JIMMY: 'Er, what would you do if you had two bikes?'
> DRUNK: 'Aw, now that's not fair, Jimmy. You know I've got two bikes . . .'

Later, the conversation drifted into another familiar dimension.

> DRUNK: 'You should have been in here last night, Jim . . .'

JIMMY: 'Warr'appened?'

DRUNK: 'You should have been here, pal. A feller came in selling cigs. Woodies – ten bob a million.

JIMMY: 'You should have got me twenty.'

It's odd that a few scoops of ale always make Scousers prone to exaggeration. Especially just after Christmas, when competition creeps in about who had the biggest dinner:

'You should have seen the size of our turkey. We had to run over it with a wagon. Four and a half hundredweight. We got thirty bob for the bones . . .'

One of the first things you notice about Liverpool pubs is the fact that all the big fellers want to sing, and all the little fellers want to fight. In between, the talk goes on and on . . .

'Nice dogs, them, pal. Jack Russell's, are they?'

'No, they're our kid's.'

Or:

'Did I tell you our house was broken into last night? The police rang this morning to say they'd got the feller. I told them to ask him how he got in without waking the wife.'

Anything reported in the *Liverpool Echo* is always a source of gossip. Unfortunately the stories grow taller with the telling.

'Did you read about that feller in your street trying to hang himself? The cops found him swinging with a rope round his waist.'

'Shouldn't it have been round your neck?' they asked him.

'It was,' he said, 'But it was chokin' me.'

Wending your way safely home can be a dodgy business. My cousin, who had had a scoop or three, was

*Singing for my supper.*

weaving along the pavement. Two nuns approached him and, as they drew nearer, parted and passed on either side of him.

'Jeez,' he said, whirling round. 'How did you do that, Sister?'

Scousers find it impossible to come home quietly from a pub. At two in the morning, wives have to face the prospect of twenty-five men stamping up the garden path, trying to kill the hosepipe.

Then, there is the rattling on the door.

'Mrs Jones?'

'Yes.'

'Can you tell us which one's your Charlie, so the rest of us can go home?'

Of course, the following morning they pay the price with a gigantic hangover. A friend of mine lurched into the chemist's in his lunch hour and said:

'Me head's killing me. It's been on and off all morning. Give me the strongest thing you've got.'

'Well, sir,' the chemist said. 'Nothing acts faster than Anadin.'

'That's the one,' my pal said. 'Give me a box of nothin'.'

There is nothing quite as sharp as Scouse wit. And, just when you think things are going well, it takes a Liverpudlian to bring you down to earth. This was brought home to me in 1980 when I joined the *Canberra* for a working cruise. I was standing in the ballroom when a little old lady from Childwall walked past and noticed me out of the corner of her eye.

She skidded to a halt and did a double take: 'It's Tom O'Connor,' she said excitedly. 'Could you just wait there one minute, Tom, while I run down to my cabin and get my camera?'

I gave her a nice smile and smoothed down my hair and straightened my tie. In no time at all she scuttled back with her camera and shoved it at me.

'Just look through the little hole, and press that button there, Tom,' she said, and stepped back into a pose.

At the time I embarked on my first cruise, I had made four live LP's of my stage act. The brainwave struck me that, if there were, say, a thousand passengers on the ship, they might each buy one. The result of this brilliant piece of enterprise was a total sale of three.

Now, if you can imagine the weight of 997 LP's, you will know why it took four blokes to carry the trunk through customs on the way back into Britain.

And, sure enough, the customs man who singled me out was a Scouser. He checked the suitcases, and I told him I had nothing to declare.

'What's in the trunk, then?' he asked.

'Oh, just a few records.'

'Okay. Open it up.'

The four men carried it, heaving and grunting, over to the customs counter, where the Scouse officer threw back the lid.

'All yours, are they?'

'That's correct.'

'Collect records, do you?'

'You could say that,' I replied, trying my best to forget the whole disastrous venture.

He pulled out one record, then another, and yet another.

'They're all the same,' he said, examining the covers. 'They're all by you . . .'

'That's right.'

'Okay,' said the customs officer, throwing down the lid. 'On yer way.'

As we staggered out of the shed gasping under our baggage, he could not resist expressing his thoughts. 'Big head,' he called after me.

On rare occasions, Scousers have been known to score an own-goal. The most memorable was a well-known Liverpool comedian, who unfortunately has to remain nameless. Years ago – and this is an absolutely true story – he was booked into a club in Manchester at 11pm. He arrived two hours early and, to kill time, decided to go for a drink in another club, a few doors down the street.

The comedian had hardly got inside the door when there was trouble. He was not a member and, after an argument, a twenty-stone bouncer gave him a smack and threw him onto the pavement.

The Scouser retreated to a nearby pub to lick his wounds and, as each pint went down, grew more livid about the way he had been treated. He figured that, by midnight, he would be out of town. As no one knew him in Manchester, he could go back and fix the bouncer without any recrimination.

Slowly, he worked out his plan. Next door there was a snooker hall – the comedian walked in, stole a billiard ball and headed up the road. Outside the club, he took off his shoe, put the heavy ball in the toe of his sock and knocked on the club door.

When the bouncer opened it, he swung back the sock. Almost immediately there was a clunk as the billiard ball slipped through a hole in the toe, and landed on the floor behind his back. The comedian wacked with all his might and flopped the bouncer over the nose with an empty, smelly sock. The bouncer looked puzzled for a moment then, to be on the safe side, knocked out two of the comic's front teeth.

Liverpudlians are as unique as their humour. Each

*Royal Variety Show, Liverpool Empire, 1978 – who gave Doddy the lemon?*

Scouse entertainer has had his own distinctive style –
Billy Bennett, Ted Ray, Arthur Askey, Rob Wilton, Ken
Dodd, Jimmy Tarbuck. Yet strangely, no one knew that
the early stars came from Merseyside. None of them
admitted to it until Frankie Vaughan came along. He
made it clear right from the start, and others began to
follow suit.

I am sure it had something to do with traditional
Scouse secretiveness – the same trait which makes
dockers hide behind nicknames and people in the street
instinctively answer a question with a question:

'Is this the bus stop?'

'Are you going to town?'

Or:

'Is this the Empire?'

'Why, are you on there?'

I have been caught so many times by this that I once
decided to beat them at their own game. I planted myself
in front of a post office window and asked a Scouser: 'Is
this the post office?'

It would be difficult for anyone not to give a straight
answer, but he replied: 'Are you buying stamps?'

My wife, Pat, who comes from Yorkshire, first noticed
this. East of the Pennines, a man stands at a bar and talks
about what he has done. In Liverpool you walk into a
pub, and a Scouser's opening remark is: 'Hello, mate.
Where are you from?' By the end of the evening you have
told him your entire life story and left, without ever
knowing his name.

Liverpool's rich seam of comic talent, Arthur Askey
believed, is rooted in the fact that, originally, there were
so many music halls – later clubs and theatre clubs – that
there was opportunity for everyone to try his hand.

There were also visiting stars. Comedian Issy Bonn

played pantomime and always tried to pack in plugs for himself. So, when Aladdin rubbed the lamp and the Genie said: 'You may have any wish you desire,' his reply was: 'I wish to hear Issy Bonn sing his latest record "Goldmine In The Sky".'

'It shall be granted . . .'

Liverpool Club secretaries were a law unto themselves. They made a point of never passing a complimentary remark, even if you had brought the house down. The habit was so ingrained in some of them that they could deflate performers even as they were walking through the door.

I remember Eric Delaney and his band arriving at one club, to be greeted by the secretary.

'Evenin', Eric,' he said. 'Have you brought your own drummer, or do you want to use Albert?'

Entertainers from outside Merseyside often failed to get a measure of their audience. One comic died on his feet. 'I can't understand it,' he said when he came off. 'My jokes must have gone straight over their heads.'

'Well, it's too late to lower the speakers now,' the compère replied.

I was fortunate to have a big Liverpudlian following and Scousers, being what they are, always try to look after their own. Around 1970 I had just bought a new Fiat 124, and found myself at the Eagle and Child pub in Kirkby – Huyton Country Club, as it is locally known.

I was quite proud of the car and was standing with my back to the bar, keeping my eye on it through the front window. The bloke next to me, a Chinese Liverpudlian, caught me guarding it and asked: 'Are those Pirelli Cinturano tyres?'

'As a matter of fact they are,' I said, wondering what was coming next.

'Do you want another set?' he asked.

'Why, can you get some?'

My interest was roused because, at the time, they were an astronomical price.

'Fifteen quid for a set of five,' he offered.

I could hardly believe it.

'Do you work at the tyre factory?' I asked him.

'No,' he said. 'But I start in the morning.'

Sooner or later, wherever you travel in the world, you will bump into a member of the International Scouse Mafia. Liverpudlians always seem to be in minor positions of authority – not, I hasten to say, because they are on the fiddle – but it is a funny coincidence, nevertheless. When I was at college in London, the President of the Union was a Scouser, along with the entire canteen staff and the men who filled the cigarette and coffee machines.

When I joined the *Canberra*, I flew to Sydney and fell into bed in my cabin with jet lag. The next morning there was a note under the door.

'Dear Tom, there is a pan of scouse on the stove. Knock second door left.'

And, sure enough, there was. Half the galley crew were from Liverpool.

The story which illustrates this camaraderie beyond any other is one which fills me with horror whenever I think of it. Even now, I tell it with great reluctance, wondering if the long arm of the law will still descend on someone.

Early in my career, I won *Opportunity Knocks* three times in succession – a feat which prompted Hughie Green to take me to one side and remark:

'We've never seen anything like this before, Tom. Sacksful of votes have been pouring in for you. The remarkable thing is that every vote we've had from

Merseyside has been for you, and nobody else on the show.'

I was naturally pleased, until a couple of years later, when I was playing the She Club in Liverpool. After my spot, in the early hours of the morning, I went to the bar for a pint. Next to me there was a postman, sitting on a bar stool in full uniform, with a delivery bag over his shoulder.

He had popped in from the city's main sorting office around the corner in Victoria Street and, like all Scousers, felt obliged to explain why he was having a pint during working hours.

'I'm entitled to this, you know,' was his opening remark. 'I'm on me break.'

We fell into conversation and, a couple of pints later, he gave me a wink and said: 'Aye. We looked after you on *Opportunity Knocks*.'

'How do you mean?' I asked, puzzled.

'All them postcards voting for the others,' he explained. 'The lads sorted them out and made sure they all went in the bin . . .'

# 5  *In my Liverpool Home*

There were three types of housing in Bootle when I was a boy – terraced, prefabs and semi-condemned. There were also one or two detached homes. They had actually once been semis, but somebody had pinched the other half. You would always know when a cargo of paint had been unloaded down at the docks because, the following week, all the prefabs would be painted the same colour, bright red or emerald green.

I grew up in Spencer Street which, for reasons best known to the council, was the only street in Bootle with a tarmac surface. It was just a thin layer, but all the others were still cobbled, and I had to suffer for it at school.

From an early age it was important to differentiate between the rough kids and the 'posh' kids.

Posh kids would never take a sweet from you if it had

been in your mouth, and always collected bonfire wood with their gloves on. They came from the kind of family where the mother scrubbed the front step in a fur coat, and made bread pudding with Hovis.

Rough kids – and round our way they were rough – had to take a note into school to explain why they were there.

Most of the area had been heavily bombed in the dockland Blitz and, years later, when the tarmac bubbled in the summer heat, you could prise pieces of shrapnel from it with a penknife.

Down our way they used to say it was so rough that people took their doorsteps in at night. It hasn't changed much – last year they were twinned with Beirut. It was such a poor area when I was young that the council used to have complaints from gypsies. In our house we had so many wet nappies round the fireguard that there was a rainbow right across the lobby.

In the days of rationing after the war, I remember one of the neighbours bringing a live pig home.

'What are you going to do with that?' his wife asked.

'Keep it in the house till we need it,' he told her.

'But what about the smell?'

'Well,' the husband said, 'I suppose the pig'll have to get used to it.'

Some outsiders might have got the impression that it was a nice place to live because the butcher called four times a week. In fact, he came once with the meat, and three times for the money.

At about the age of five, we all wore those woolly mittens which were attached to each other by a piece of string which went up one sleeve and down the other. If you didn't like someone, you could jerk one end of his string and he would smack himself in the face.

It was only when I looked back years later that I pitied the rent man. There was never a single occasion when he collected money from every house in the street. Well, perhaps just one. He was jubilant – until somebody mugged him as he did a lap of honour.

At Christmas, Scousers being the way they are, family after family would invite him in for a double scotch. At the end of the day he pedalled home legless – still with an empty money bag.

When I last heard of him, he had taken early retirement and become a commando in the Salvation Army.

Anyone who fell behind with their payments ran the risk of being taken to court. One of our neighbours found herself before the magistrate for rent arrears. She was ordered to pay them off at the rate of fifty pence a week.

The following Friday, when the rentman called, she handed him fifty pence.

'What's this for?' he asked.

'We'll get the arrears out of the way first,' she said. 'Then we'll pay the rent.'

There was a community spirit which somehow never carried over to the new estates in Kirkby and Skelmersdale. It could, however, have its disadvantages. No one minded if a neighbour popped in to borrow a cup of sugar, but one woman a few doors down – Borrowing Bertha, my mother called her – took it too far.

I opened the front door one day to be greeted with: 'Can you ask your mam to rub a bit of soap on this flannel?'

Another time, she opened with: 'Do you think we could borrow your Sunday joint to make some gravy?'

I thought she had gone too far when she knocked and asked: 'Could I borrow half a pound of butter, a few currants, a bottle of milk and a bag of flour? Only, I

found a bit of soda and thought I'd make a cake . . .'

My mother always obliged, until one day she could take no more.

Bertha hammered at the door and enquired: 'Could I borrow your washing line?'

'No,' my mother told her firmly. 'I'm using it to tie up some loose sawdust.'

'You can't tie up sawdust with a washing line,' Bertha accused her.

'It's surprising what you can do with a washing line when you don't want to lend it out,' my mother said.

Scousers retain a great nostalgia for the old days. But, as the song says, times are changing:

A feller from the Corpy, straight out of planning school,
Has told us that we've got to get right out of Liverpool.
They're sending us to Kirkby, Skelmersdale or Speke.
Don't want to go from all I know in Back Buchanan Street.

I'll miss the foghorns on the river, and the auld Pier Head,
And skippin' up the jiggers when I'm rollin' home to bed.
There's lots of other things, like putting out the cat,
'Cos there's no back door on the fourteenth floor of a Corporation flat.

I'll miss the pub around the corner, with its parlour painted red,
Like I miss the green goddess and the Overhead.

*Mrs O'Connor's lad*

From Walton to the Dingle, you can hear the same old cry:
Stop messin' about with Liverpool – at least until I die.

Now I'll miss the Mary Ellen's, and me dad will miss the dock.
Me gran will miss the wash house where she washed me grandad's socks.
They'll pulled down Paddy's Market, where me Ma once had a stall,
And soon those picks and shovels will be through our back yard wall.

The men of the street were our heroes. Most of them were in the Merchant Navy and, when their ships docked, we would walk behind them imitating the Western Ocean Roll – a little like the John Wayne Sway, only tougher. They could do no wrong because they brought home the first Batman comics from America.

Our next door neighbour, One Leg Logan, would arrive home and buy the entire Top Twenty. On a Sunday, everyone carried out their chairs and sat on the pavement to talk. One Leg Logan would open his front door, turn up a radiogram the size of a double-decker bus and belt out numbers, such as *Wheel Of Fortune* by Kay Starr. Logan, who actually had two good legs, earned his nickname from these sessions. He would sit out on a chair, banging his right leg up and down in time to the music, until my dad could take no more:

'Logan,' he shouted one day. 'I'll nail that bloody foot to the floor.'

The only way he could fight back was to turn our old valve radio up to full volume. It was in the days before batteries, when kids had to run to the shop to get the accumulator topped up with acid. Usually they came home with holes burned in their trousers.

'Don't you be bouncin' about on the way back,' dads would warn. 'You'll mix all the programmes up.'

Life was one endless run to the corner shop and back again. It was a wonderful age when soap powders were called Omo and Oxydol, and toothpaste Dentifreeze. I remember it contained something called carboxyhymoglobis, which is now a disease.

Shopping is one of the few things in Liverpool which has ever changed. Now, elsewhere in Britain, people walk into a shop, give their order, perhaps talk about the weather and leave. In Liverpool it is more like the Gunfight at the OK Corral, with everyone firing from the lip.

The housewife sets out determined that no one is going to put one over on her and, faced with this artillery all day, the man behind the counter is equally determined he is not going to lose face. As soon as the bell jingles on the door, it's seconds out.

Only in a local Liverpool butcher's shop could you hear conversations such as:

'Half a pound of neck end and . . . hey, d'you know there's a sausage on the floor?'

'It's all right, love, I've got me foot on it.'

When a man goes to a butcher's with a shopping list, the smart Alec behind the counter always tries to destroy him:

'Two ounces of boiled ham, please.'

'Any invitations to the party, pal?'

If, by accident, he reads his wife's instructions, he is guaranteed to go down at the starting gate:

'Er, three pork chops, and can you make sure the fat's cut off . . .'

'They don't peel the bananas before they weigh them, you know.'

Sometimes he may manage to score a point:

'The wife's sent me for a pair of kippers.'

'We haven't got a pair.

'Well give us two odd ones. She won't notice the difference.'

Glenda Jackson, who came from Birkenhead, once said: 'Put any two Scousers together and you've got a double act.'

In all my years round the local shops, I don't think I ever saw anyone successfully complain to a Liverpool butcher. But it was not through lack of trying:

'Hey,' said one woman. 'That big leg of lamb I bought here – when it came out of the oven it was like that' – she held apart her finger and thumb.

'I had the same trouble with a sweater, love,' said the butcher. 'When I washed it, it shrunk. Must have come off the same sheep, eh?'

The only time I found a butcher lost for words was when I stood in a queue behind a woman who asked:

'Have you got a humpty-backed rabbit? I'm making a pie and I can't get the dough to rise . . .'

When a family had to tighten its belt, mothers preferred to go shopping alone in case the kids embarrassed her.

'Can I have a few of them scraps for the dog?' she would ask the butcher.

And the little lad would say: 'Oh goody, mam. Are we gettin' a dog?'

The shops themselves had to struggle to make a living. One storekeeper in Bootle could not make a profit, and was forced to think about closing down. He advertised a going-out-of-business sale, and found that it was a runaway success. The shopkeeper made so much money from it that he went out of business for the next twenty years, and bought his son a shop with the profits. The last time I passed, his son was making a fortune going out of business, too.

I loved running errands because many of the products contained free gifts. At one time I had a collection of more than a thousand 'Cricketers of 1955' cigarette cards – until it occurred to me that there couldn't possibly be so many people in the game. Who did they all play for? I lost interest at the point when I collected a picture of my Uncle Charlie. He only batted twice – the first time he was out for a duck; the second LBW, when the ball hit him on the leg and killed his ferret.

We all used to collect car numbers. I would sit against the wall and write down thousands of them in notebook after notebook. It started because a story went round school that the police were looking for a murderer, and there was five pounds reward for the first kid who spotted his car. Then one day the penny dropped – how would I know it was his car, even if I had written the number down?

As a child I used to play all the traditional Liverpool street games, such as Forwards, Backwards, Sideways. For anyone unfamiliar with this, we would hit a kid on the head with a shovel and lay bets on which way he fell over.

Summer holidays meant taking the ferry across the Mersey to New Brighton, with butties and a bottle of water. The smallest always got the last swig of the bottle – the one with all the breadcrumbs floating in it. What made it worse was that the kid who had drunk from it before him usually had purple ointment on his lip. Anyone who had to wipe the bottle on their sleeve before

*Pope John Paul II – the only person ever to fall asleep during my act.*

taking a drink wasn't tough enough to be in the gang.

Saturday mornings were spent in the Palace Cinema in Marsh Lane, known locally as the Bug House. Among my favourites were *Sabu the Elephant Boy* (by now, even the elephant has forgotten him); *Flash Gordon*, which had a soundtrack that echoed so much I believed for years it was recorded in a lavatory; and *Hopalong Cassidy*.

No one ever saw a film all the way through – the fights in the stalls were a much bigger attraction. The highlight of the morning was when the manager climbed onto the stage and warned: 'If another missile hits this screen . . .'

*Hopalong* was always greeted with a roar from the audience. The only event which received more applause that I can remember was when a lad fired a rocket from a milk bottle in the centre aisle, and it went right through the screen.

The fun for all of us was booing the baddies, cheering the goodies and, of course, booing all the girls in the film. When I say all of us, I mean with the exception of Bertie Postlethwaite. Bertie used to like the girls. We worried about Bertie. When we played Cowboys and Indians, he always wanted to be tied up. Funny chap; he's a magistrate now.

The perfect end to the Saturday matinée was to tie your mac round your neck like Zorro, and gallop home, slapping your backside. I used to hitch up my horse at the end of the street and walk along the terrace trying to look like John Wayne. My mother always thought I had wet my trousers.

Everyone was struggling to make money in those days – I remember trying to turn out pound notes with my John Bull printing set. It's interesting that, when people had nothing, they would say: 'Come on in – help yourself.' Now, when they have something, they peep at you through a hole in the door.

There were a few optimistic souls who even tried to pull the wool over the eyes of fellow Scousers. They made some brave attempts, but it never lasted.

My father, patriotic to the last, answered an advertisement which promised: 'Send me £1 and I will send you a miniature colour portrait of the King.' Back in the post came a halfpenny stamp.

On another occasion, I heard two Scousers planning to make some cash. They had found a dead donkey, and one of them had had a brainwave.

'We could raffle this donkey,' he said. 'Just think – two hundred tickets at a pound a ticket – that's two hundred quid.'

'Aye,' said his mate thoughtfully. 'But what happens when the winner finds out the donkey's dead?'

'We give him his money back.'

A Scouser's inbuilt caution makes it difficult to take advantage of him. This was demonstrated some years ago when *Candid Camera* concealed a film crew in the bushes in Sefton Park. They had been round the country offering people a five pound note for two pounds, to test their reactions.

The first Liverpudlian was approached:

INTERVIEWER: 'Excuse me. Would you like to buy a fiver for two pounds? It's a genuine bargain . . .'

There was a short, suspicious pause as the gears of Liverpudlian logic engaged.

SCOUSER: 'Okay. We'll split the difference. Just give me three quid and we'll call it straight.'

Times may have been hard, but Liverpudlians always try to make sure they have life's little necessities. I remember when colour television first came out, a family from our street went straight down to the local TV shop.

'I want a telly,' the father said. 'One of them new coloured ones. The biggest you've got.'

'Certainly, sir,' the salesman said. 'We have a good model here with quadrophonic sound and a giant screen – the best on the market – at £2,000.'

'Wrap it up,' said the father. 'We'll take it.'

'Will you be paying cash, or HP?'

'HP, naturally.'

'Well, we will have to run a check on your finances, sir . . .'

'That's OK, pal,' the father told him. 'I'm earnin' £200 a week at Ford's, and the wife brings home £100 a week sweepin' the factory floor.'

When they arrived home the father lost no time buttonholing the children:

'Listen, you lot. If a feller knocks at the door and asks where your mam and dad are, tell him that I'm out earnin' £200 a week at Ford's, and your mam's brushin' the shop floor for £100 a week. Got it?'

The next morning the door-knocker rattled, and the little boy answered it.

'Is your father in?' the caller asked.

'No,' the lad recited dutifully. 'He's out at work earnin' £200 a week, and me mam's brushin' up to bring home £100 a week.'

'I see,' said the caller. 'Well, when they get home, will you tell them that the man from the Social Security would like to have a word with them?'

The shadow of the finance company fell over everyone. One family received the following letter:

Dear Sir,
 You have a dining suite, a bedroom suite, a washing

machine and a colour television on which you have not yet made a single payment. Unless you take steps to rectify this, we shall be forced to repossess them.

Hoping it would add some leverage, the finance company concluded:
'If this happened, what would your neighbours think?'
The man who received the letter wrote back:

Dear Sir,
  I have had a word with the neighbours, and they think it would be a lousy trick.

In every house in the street there were certain weekly rituals. At around eight o'clock on a Friday night you could hear all the front doors opening and husbands calling: 'I'm off to the alehouse – if the pools feller calls, the money's behind the clock.'
Wives seldom went with them, and some never went out at all. My Auntie Minnie was one of the band who always lived in hope. She would sit all day in her curlers, with a pair of her husband's socks on, and her legs like corned beef from the gas fire. When he came home she was like a goddess – completely transformed. But an hour later, after a quick wash, the door would slam and he would be off for a night out with his mates.
'He never takes me nowhere,' Auntie Minnie would moan. 'There's just me an' these four walls. Me window's me world . . .'
One Saturday morning her husband proved her wrong. At half-past six he nudged her in the ribs, and said: 'Are you coming to the strike meeting, or what?'
It turned out to be a union rally in London. One of the highlights of the trip was a visit to Speakers' Corner. On

the first soap box stood an ugly-looking preacher with a face like a bagful of hammers; his nose was going north and his ears going south.

'I see we have some new faces in the crowd today,' he said.

'Then why don't you grab yourself one, pal?' Uncle Billy shouted.

When the strike meeting was on he gave her a handful of notes and told her to buy herself a new dress for Christmas.

'Now listen,' Billy warned. 'It's not like the Pool down here. They'll try to diddle you. Don't be payin' an arm and a leg for a bit of dishcloth. Whatever they ask, halve it.'

Auntie Minnie nodded and set off. In Knightsbridge she picked out a dress and asked the shop manager how much it cost.

'Two hundred guineas, madame.'

'I'll give you a hundred,' Minnie offered.

The manager was a little flustered.

'We don't haggle or reduce prices here, madam,' he said quietly.

'My Billy was right,' Minnie shouted. 'You're all bloody robbers . . .'

'Madam,' said the manager, embarrassed. 'Please calm down. If it will make you happy, one hundred.'

'You must think we were born yesterday,' said Minnie. 'I'll give you fifty.'

'Madam, I beg you,' said the manager, lowering his voice to a whisper. 'All right, fifty.'

'Twenty-five.'

'Look. If you promise to leave the shop now, you can have the dress for nothing . . .'

'I want two,' Minnie told him.

# 6  *Matches and Despatches*

When someone in our street died, there was never a dull moment. Or, as they used to say: 'Where there's a will, there's an argument . . .' Bereavements, like weddings, bring out the worst in everyone.

A pal of my grandad went out in classic Scouse style. He had just climbed onto the table at the billiard hall to get a tricky black in the corner pocket, when his foot slipped and down he went. His mates only sensed something was wrong when they went through his pockets for the money for the next round, and he didn't flinch.

The following evening there was a knock at his front door:

'Er, Mrs Jones? I've come from work. I'm a mate of Tommy's – thought I'd pay my respects.'

'Oh. Thank you.'

'Were you with him when he went?'

'Yes, I was,' she said, wringing her pinny.

'Er, he didn't happen to mention a tin of green paint, did he?'

'Well, no. He didn't, actually.'

'Did he say anything about a set of box spanners and a foot pump?'

'He never mentioned them . . .'

'That's all right. I'll hang onto them, then.'

Years ago everyone would have a three-part bereavement. The body would be laid out in the coffin in the front room, the young ones would be dancing in the middle room, while all the old ones sat round the kitchen drinking Guinness.

The conversation generally drifted into such deep thoughts as:

'You get older every day, don't you?'

'One thing's sure – you can't take it with you.'

'Aye, there's no pockets in a shroud.'

'Hmm. They reckon the good always go first.'

'I know, I haven't been feeling too well meself lately.'

After a few scoops the women would make their way to the front room to pay their last respects.

'Aw, God – doesn't he look happy?'

'He died in his sleep, and doesn't know he's dead yet.'

'Jeez, if he wakes up in the morning, the shock'll kill him.'

Before long it is time for the funeral, but the all-important travel arrangements have to be made:

'Now with regard to the funeral procession,' the man of the house announces, 'I've got that fixed up. We can only afford one car for the immediate family – that's me and the wife. But the rest of you can get a 58 bus round

the corner. Or, alternatively, you can cut across the brick field.'

'What about the old folk?' someone asks.

'Well, right, I'm coming to that. For the benefit of the old people – right – who can't make the bus stop, don't worry. I've arranged for the hearse to make a second run.'

Modern funerals are, of course, completely different. The pace of life is getting quicker, and the speed at which they move is frightening. The drivers of today's under-taker's cars look as though they are practising for a getaway from a bank raid. Half the bereaved turn up in taxis and tell them to wait with the meter ticking over.

Life's other milestone, courtship and marriage, is a unique ritual in Liverpool. The best place to meet a girl used to be a local dancehall – the Grafton, the Locarno, Orrell Park Ballroom – or even a cruise up the Mersey on the *Royal Iris*, the floating fish and chip shop. When rock and roll was the rage I would spend all week learning to jive holding the doorknob.

It was generally a waste of time, because the girls danced with each other, while the blokes stood ten deep at the bar, waiting for the last waltz.

'D'you come here often?' she would ask as you tried to figure out the footwork.

'Don't ask me – I'm counting.'

Nowadays, in discos, everything is much more aban-doned. People just shuffle around and shout:

'Can I have the last dance with you?' the lad asks.

'Yer avin' it.'

'What colour's your back door?'

'Green. But you'll never see it.'

When the courting becomes serious, couples like to get

*Panto days in Scotland*

out of the city for a picnic. Now, the countryside is one place where Scousers are out of their element. One lad and his girlfriend, for instance, were eating their butties on Bidston Hill:

'Hold on. Don't move,' he warned her in mid-mouthful.

'What's the matter?'

'There's a very dangerous fly buzzing round your face. Keep still.'

'Oo-er. What is it?'

'It looks like a dum-dum fly . . .'

'Mother of God,' said the girl, freezing. 'What's a dum-dum fly?'

'It's something that hangs around the back end of cows,' her boyfriend answered.

'Hang on,' she said indignantly. 'Are you inferrin' that my face is like the back end of a cow?'

'It's nothin' to do with me, love,' her boyfriend said. 'But you'll have to convince that fly.'

When a young man's fancy lightly turns to thoughts of marriage, proposals on bended knee are strictly out in Liverpool. It is more a case of the hand-in-pocket-walk-up-and-down style.

'D'you wanna get married, or what?'

'I'm not very good looking.'

'That's all right. You'll be at work all day.'

'Will you let me work, then?'

'I'm relyin' on it.'

'Where we goin' to live?'

'Over a pawnshop. You wanna be near your wedding ring, don't you?'

Romance may be dead, but Scousers have never been afraid to expand their horizons. Our kid married a girl from over the water – Birkenhead, to be exact. It took her a while to adjust to cooking. At first she used to spend days trying to make chips with Smash.

When they settled in they invited me round for a meal. Unfortunately, the instructions on the packet of peas said, 'Boil Separately', and we had to wait eight hours for dinner. When it finally arrived, I thought there was a peculiar taste to it.

'It must be chicken,' his wife said. 'It was burned when I took it out of the oven, so I rubbed some Vaseline on it.'

They seem a happy couple, though.

'Until I married, I was my own worst enemy,' our kid always says.

The secret of a happy marriage is sticking together in sickness and in health. It can be particularly testing time if you have been booked into hospital for an operation. I remember it playing on my father's mind for days and, of course, watching operations on television didn't help.

'You know why they wear those masks, don't you?' he kept saying as the day drew nearer. 'It's so you can't recognize them . . .'

On the morning he was due to go, he lay in bed, too terrified to get up.

'I can't go through with it,' he told my mother. 'Ring the hospital. Tell them I'm sick.'

'You get on that bus with your pyjamas,' she said. 'There's nothing wrong with you . . .'

The strain of wedding days, on reflection, is enough to put anyone in hospital. Tension sets in early – mother has been up all morning hoovering, father has a bad back from bending over the kitchen table cutting sandwiches, and the salad has been ready on the table for a week.

At the church, chaos prevails as the ushers try to sort out the seating:

'Excuse me, are you a friend of the groom?'

*Before I passed my driving test*

'Certainly not, I'm the bride's mother.'

By the time they come out of church, the pubs are open, and there is already an air of impatience. The photographer is regarded merely as someone standing in the way of the first round.

'Just take one big one,' they tell him. 'You can cut it up later.'

Back at the house, for the reception, there is always a strict pecking order of seating, according to which family you belong to. Some poor guest no sooner sits down before a voice says:

'What are you doing on the corned beef table? You're up on the boiled ham table with our lot. Hey,' he shouts to someone else. 'Her crowd are on the potted meat. Move them all down . . .'

All the knives and forks have little pieces of string tied to them to indicate who has lent them. And if someone happens to drop a china cup, a dozen heads duck under the table to see which one of them it belongs to.

At the end of the meal everyone adjourns to the pub to drink steadily from half-past-five until closing time. The danger period at any Liverpool wedding approaches as the bar towels go up and the clock creeps round to eleven. The fight could start any minute now, and the women know it.

They steer their husbands back to the reception with a firm hand, warning them: 'You keep your mouth shut. You were bad enough at me dad's funeral, you.'

In the kitchen the crates of Guinness are produced and Uncle Jimmy decides to toast the bride and groom. He was drunk at a quarter-to-one and, by now, he is out of his mind:

'Well, I'd like to propose all the best to the happy couple. Now, I know the lad very well, he's my favourite nephew. The girl *seems* a nice girl, despite the family of snides she comes from. And I'm sure, if he tries hard enough, he'll make an honest girl out of her.'

In a flash the bride's mother is on her feet:

'Don't you say a word about her. She's my werld, that girl. If the truth's known, she's too good for that lad.'

Instantly, the bridegroom's mother is up:

'Listen here, curtain hair. You want the truth? I'll tell you the truth. Your daughter told lies so she could marry my son. It wasn't him at all.'

The next thing, the whole room is up — forty of them killing each other. In go the heads, the Timpsons, and all the time one bloke at the back of the fight is shouting:

'Mind the ale, lads. Mind the ale . . .'

When the police van arrives, bringing the final guests of any Scouse party, there are bodies everywhere. Broken glasses, blood on the floor.

'All right, what's the trouble?'

'No trouble here, officer,' says the bride's mother. 'We were just doing the hokey-cokey and we all bumped into each other . . .'

# 7 Dr Christian Barnard meets Harry the Horse

There are three major sports in Liverpool – football, rugby and job hunting. Work, depending on your outlook, can be a curse or a blessing. There was a time when even the mere mention of certain places of employment implied El Dorado. The name alone was enough – nothing more need be said:

'How's your kid?'

'He's doing all right. He's at Ford's.'

For all we know he might have been brewing tea, or brushing the shop floor. But, above all, a man could walk tall when he worked on the docks. Dockers, more than even football and the Beatles, summed up the spirit of Liverpool – tough men with a fast answer and an eye peeled for an opportunity.

The only time a docker ran to work, they used to say,

was when there was a rum boat in. Despite the fact that Liverpool dockers were the best in the world, it is amazing how many crates were accidentally smashed in the course of a day.

Scousers could always tell, for instance, when there was a sugar boat in – you could stand a spoon up in the tea in the dockers' canteen. Every mug was three feet high with sugar.

Once, for the *Tom O'Connor Show*, we took a camera down to a Dock Road café, and asked the first docker we met to describe the oddest cargo he had ever unloaded. The café, incidentally, was just the kind that dockers love. Where the service was superb – 'if you can't smell it, we haven't got it' – and you could be on your fourth bowl of soup before you realized the roof was leaking.

The old docker told a story about clearing a hold and finding a wooden cask in the corner.

'Listen, lads,' one of the gang said. 'It's got to have ale in it. Let's just give it a tap and find out.'

The lid of the cask was accidentally smashed, as these things happen, and one of them experimentally dipped his finger in.

'Well, it's not ale,' he said, sucking it. 'But it's definitely alcohol.'

There was a mad scramble for the canteen on the quay. Minutes later they were back with paper cups and orange squash to dilute the exotic beverage.

'Hey, this is the stuff,' they laughed, knocking them back.

Half an hour later the entire gang were not only well-oiled, but more drunk than they had ever been. No one noticed a van draw up alongside the ship. On the side of it read 'Liverpool School Of Tropical Medicine', and a man in a white coat trotted up the companionway.

82

'Any of you lads come across our pickled monkey?' he asked.

The docker I interviewed claimed he was none the worse for drinking formaldehyde, but he did have a huge red nose, the size of a triffid.

Americans were fascinated by Liverpool in the Sixties. They poured into the city to catch up with what was happening, soaking up the atmosphere and photographing anything that moved. When one tourist saw a crowd gathered round a docker writhing in agony on the pavement outside Alexander Dock, he was curious.

'What's the matter with that guy?' he asked.

The docker rolled around moaning, with his hands thrust between his legs.

'He wants to go to the gents,' one of them said.

'Well, why doesn't he just go?' the American asked, puzzled.

'What – in his lunch hour?'

Now, I would never suggest that dockers were always on the fiddle, but there was one thing I noticed from an early age. When a business man held up his copy of the *Liverpool Echo* to flag down a bus, it would often sail past ignoring him. When a docker wanted to stop a bus he would step off the kerb in front of it. The driver would slam on his brakes for the simple reason that if he hit the docker there would be tins of salmon rolling all over the Commercial Road.

It always reminds me of the story of the docker walking out of the gate with a pumpkin under his arm:

'Where are you going with that under your arm?' the policeman asked.

And the docker said: 'Oh God, it isn't midnight already, is it?'

Dock gate policemen have to be ready for anything.

One of them was sitting in his hut when a docker ran out of the dock and up the road as fast an Olympic contender. The policeman sprinted after him, made a flying rugby tackle and brought him to the floor. He searched all the fugitive's pockets, inside and out, and was puzzled to find nothing.

'They're all empty,' the policeman said.

'I know,' said the docker. 'I'm just checking my handicap for tomorrow.'

In the past a lot was made of the odd missing bottle of scotch, or tin of fruit, simply because they were Scousers. It was rather like the coach trip to Woburn Safari park when a little boy was seen being mauled by a lion. A man jumped off the coach, butted the beast and laid it completely out. Someone following in a car ran across to him and said: 'That was wonderful. You're a hero. I'm from the Press – which part of the South are you from?'

'I'm not from the South,' the man said. 'I'm a Scouser.'

Next morning the headline read: LIVERPOOL HOOLIGAN TORTURE'S CHILD'S PET.

Workers helped themselves in other parts of the country, but little was made of it. I remember hearing about an old man in a Lancashire mining village outside Wigan. The Coal Board inspector, with his bowler hat and briefcase, called at the miner's cottage on official business:

'We're investigating reports that your husband has been stealing coal from the pit,' he told the man's wife when she opened the door.

'Don't be ridiculous,' she said. 'My husband is as honest as the day is long. He's down the garden now – why don't you have a word with him?'

'I will,' the inspector said firmly.

As he disappeared round the side of the house, the

miner's wife called: 'It's a bit of a walk. If you want to save your legs, use the conveyor belt.'

Liverpool dockers made their mark on history on 21 June 1876, when they unloaded a crate containing the first live gorilla ever seen in Britain. To Victorian Scousers it must have seemed a mythical monster.

There was a story going round for many years that the gorilla broke loose and headed into the city centre. Two dockers were running down Lime Street, when a passer-by asked them what was the matter.

'There's a giant ape on the rampage,' they called.

'Which way is it going?'

'You don't think we're chasing it, do you?'

Their wit is all the sharper for being spontaneous. In the late 1970s, when refugees were pouring out of Vietnam, a ship tied up at Liverpool:

'What have you got aboard?' a docker called up to the deck.

'Vietnamese refugees,' the bosum shouted.

'Loose, or on pallets?' the docker asked.

As they made their way into Britain and a new life, his mate watched them go and commented: 'God knows what their chips will be like . . .'

Life on the docks had a pace of its own – when ten dockers pulled a boat in, and the rope snapped, none of them ever fell over. I worked on North 1 Gladstone as a cotton skin, or cargo sampler. We had to clock on at seven in the morning, but work could not start until the dockers arrived. The dockers would get there at seven-thirty, and have a tea-break until eight. Our tea-break was scheduled from eight to eight-thirty, so it was at least two hours into the day before anyone was ready for work.

One summer morning in the silly season, a TV crew

*Mr and Mrs O'Connor – newlyweds*

arrived, looking for something to make a light-hearted item for the news. The producer approached the foreman and said:

'Do you think we could persuade one of the dockers to undress and streak through the shed?'

'Listen pal,' said the foreman wearily. 'These fellers are earning £200 a week, and I can't even get them to take their overcoats off . . .'

At the time, they were unloading a ship called the *Rena del Mar*, which had run aground on a reef, and had to have its cargo of cotton bales thrown overboard to refloat. The cargo was later recovered, but it smelled to high heaven. One old docker, who had a bad chest, could not stand the fumes and stayed in the loft of the shed all day. We kept him supplied with cups of tea, and he earned the nickname The Sick Pigeon.

There were never any clothes suitable for dock work because, from one day to another, no one ever knew what type of cargo they would be handling. A docker could find himself running the risk of anthrax carrying hides, or breathing in dust from bulk flour. The men I worked alongside earned every penny.

A bonus might be paid for working in unhygienic conditions, but it had to be fought for. One ship I worked on was being unloaded when a big rat ran across the hold.

'That's it, lads,' said the foreman. 'Everybody off. We want vermin pay.'

Ten minutes later a jeep screamed across the quay carrying the bosses.

'Why has the job stopped?' they demanded.

'We want infestation money.'

'Okay,' the boss sighed. 'An extra ten bob a day, and a cat.'

'No chance,' the foreman told him. 'We want a pound a day and the Pied Piper.'

The Pen, or labour pool, which my father lived through, was little more than a cattle market, as men competed with each other for work. Many would place a half-crown on their shoulder in the hope that the foreman would pick them out.

'Right, we'll have you,' he would say, slapping them on the shoulder, and picking up the half-crown at the same time. I lost count of the times my father pawned his watch and walked miles looking for work. It was such hardship as this that honed the dockers' wit.

'Hey you, over here,' the foreman said to one docker. 'I've a job for you. Get the handcart and deliver this load of timber.'

The gang unloaded a couple of tons of timber on the cart, and the docker could hardly lift it. He set off for the dock gate, resting every ten paces.

'I forgot to mention,' called the foreman. 'When you see the feller, tell him he got Tottenham Hotspur in the draw.'

The docker went on his way, staggering and stopping under the weight of the load. By the time he knocked on the door it was almost midnight.

'Delivery,' he said. 'And the foreman said to tell yer that you've got Tottenham in the draw,' he told the customer.

'Do you know who got Nottingham Forest?'

'Me,' said the shattered docker. 'It's right here on this barrer.'

The docker's habit of giving each other nicknames lightened the working day, and provided an anonymity which they liked. Here are a few of the ones I came across over the years:

There was The Destroyer – by the middle of the week he was always looking for a sub.

Harry The Horse was never off his bike. The name stuck when a docker asked the foreman if he knew where Harry was.

'I haven't seen head nor tail of him all day,' he replied.

There was The Blister, who only showed up when the work was over.

The Gardener, who was in charge of a gang, and fond of ordering:

'Plant that one here, lads,' or 'Plant that over there.'

Anyone who could not take the tough pace was a likely target. The Jigsaw earned his nickname because, whenever he was given a difficult job he went to pieces.

Then there was Peter Pan – 'one more mistake and he's out the window . . .'

The Lazy Solicitor, who was always asleep on a case.

And a foreman called The Sheriff – 'What's the hold-up, fellers? What's the hold-up?'

My father, the only Liverpool docker with a straight hook, was a quay foreman. He was known as Our Lady of Sorrows because of a habit of pleading, 'Hey, men . . .'

No one could escape being given a label. I know one docker who managed to get a job on the South End docks for his pal.

'Now listen,' he advised him on the first day. 'As soon as you open your mouth, they'll give you a nickname. Say nothin'.'

His mate managed to remain silent all day, and was henceforth known as The Quiet Man.

Another docker I knew hated putting his hand in his pocket in the pub at lunchtime. He was soon dubbed Harvey Smith – 'another clear round,' his mates would say.

He was matched only by The Baldy Rabbit, who always had the same excuse on the bus going home: 'Lend us a tanner. I've lost me fur.'

I remember, too, the light-fingered docker they called Batman – 'he never leaves a ship without robbin'.

The Spaceman – 'I'm goin' to ma's for me dinner.'

And Diesel – 'Diesel do for our kid, diesel do for me dad . . .'

Even the policemen on the dock gates were given nicknames. One of them was Dr Christian Barnard. When the pilfering looked bad on his record sheet, he used to plead: 'Have a heart, lads . . .'

The policeman who shared the hut with him was known as The Sad Balloon – his catchphrase was: 'Don't let me down, fellers . . .'

Backache was, unsurprisingly, a common ailment on the docks, and the favourite remedy was a week off work 'on the club'. Having signed on for sickness benefit, it was tempting to take advantage of the holiday for as long as possible. As the weeks drew on, it became a war of wits convincing the doctor that you were suffering from something serious enough to keep you from work.

'I'm afraid you'll have to go back, Mr Mack,' a GP told one old docker. 'You've run the full gamut of illnesses known to medical science since World War I. According to your card, you started with shell-shock and went right through to chronic stress brought on by the FA Cup.'

The doctor took his pen and drew a line across the space on the medical certificate which read 'Nature Of Illness'.

The old docker didn't give up easily. He took it into the dock office and said: 'I'm in a bad way. The doctor's still signing me on.'

'No he isn't,' said the boss, examining the certificate. 'There's nothing wrong with you.'

'Read that, then,' said the docker jabbing his finger at 'Nature Of Illness'.

'What does it say?' the boss asked, squinting at it.

'A stroke,' the old feller told him.

The best approach was always to plead some general condition, in the hope that the doctor would play safe and prescribe treatment. Occasionally the technique backfired:

'I need something to make me sweat, Doc,' one docker pleaded.

The doctor picked up his pen and signed him back to work.

Some of the roots of Liverpool humour can be traced to World War II. The city was heavily bombed but, unlike other ports, rebuilding was slow. In Hamburg, for instance, people were moved into emergency accommodation while a showpiece city rose from the ashes.

In Liverpool, streets still had bombed houses twenty years after the war. People pulled together and coped with adversity with a quip and a quick reply.

Dockers played their part in the war effort. My grandad, in the Home Guard, was given the job of guarding the Dock Road single-handed – a feat five hundred policemen now find difficult to achieve.

'We've heard a rumour that German paratroops have landed on Merseyside,' the sergeant told him one night. 'We think they are over in New Brighton. Now keep a look-out, 'cos when the fair shuts they might come over here.'

A curfew was imposed, with strict orders to shoot anyone seen out on the streets after eleven at night. A few

*O'Connell Street, Dublin, 1948*

hours later a lone figure was staggering along the Dock Road, drunk.

'Who goes there?' called Grandad.

'Jimmy Green,' the lone voice said.

And, without further hesitation, Grandad squeezed the trigger and shot him.

'That was very good,' said the sergeant, 'but, you know, it's only quarter-to-eleven.'

'Aye,' said Grandad. 'But I know where he lives – he'd never have made it home.'

No one knew where they would be fighting next. Some Liverpudlians were drafted into the Bankers Brigade. The regimental motto was 'No Advance Without Security', and it was tough in front-line action. They all had orders to shout to the enemy: 'Can you stand still? These bullets cost money.'

Today there is just as much humour, despite the unemployment – a far cry from the years when we all saw the dole in a different light. Those were the days when Our Kid had a cauliflower ear from lying in bed. I remember him joining the Dole Protection Society. He paid twenty pence a week, and they fought his case if he was offered a job.

Down at the pub you could hear conversations such as:

'No, I'll get these – you're working.'

Or:

'Nice weather, isn't it?'

'Yeah. If I had a job, I'd take a week off.'

There was generally a more relaxed attitude. When you signed on, you would go down to the dole in Renshaw Street for a brief interview:

'What's your name?'

'John – or Jack.'

'Where do you live?'

'Here and there.'

'What jobs have you done?'

'This and that.'

'Fine. Sign this, and we'll see you now and again.'

Liverpudlians have had a bad Press. They are, in fact, the hardest workers anywhere in Britain. One typical Scouser took a job laying drains and, on his first day, was told to dig a six-foot deep trench. After lunch the boss came back and found that it was three miles long.

'That's incredible,' he said. 'You've worked like a Trojan and done that all on your own. We'll have to get you a JCB.'

'Never mind the medals,' Scouse said. 'Just get somebody to help me.'

Building sites, of course, are full of Irish labourers and, with the family coming from the Old Country, I can't agree with all the things said about them. If Scousers need time to size up a situation, the Irish simply need a little longer.

There was a lad from County Clare who started on a site and was told to work in the trench. He jumped in and fell forty feet to the bottom.

'What did you do that for?' the foreman asked. 'Why didn't you use the ladder?'

'I thought that was for going up,' he called.

Nowadays, business is slack everywhere. I took a cab in Liverpool recently and the driver told me that no one had been sick in the back for six months.

The economic situation is driving people to crime. I read a case in the *Liverpool Echo* of someone stealing £50,000.

'Can you give us any reason why you did this?' the judge asked.

The man in the dock thought for a moment, and said: 'I was hungry.'

There is now every chance of someone answering their front door to a man with a briefcase, who opens up with:

'Good morning, I'm from Littlewoods.'

'Great,' they say. 'Have we won the pools?'

'No, your daughter's been arrested for shoplifting . . .'

Some Scousers are even being forced to travel abroad to seek their fortunes, but the accent has been known to pose problems. Imagine, for instance, a Liverpudlian waiter in the elegant surroundings of the Rome Hilton:

' . . . We've got ravioli – that's, like er, teabags in tomato sauce. And here's a mug of tea to put you on. Do you take sugar?'

'No.'

'Well don't stir it, then.'

'Waiter,' another diner calls. 'There's something funny about this steak.'

'Well laugh at it.'

'Waiter,' someone else beckons, snapping their fingers at him.

'Listen, Jim,' he warns. 'Do you wanna wake up with a crowd round yer?'

One Scouser, unable to take any more of dole and domestic life, actually ran away to join the Foreign Legion.

'Why do you want to enlist?' the recruiting sergeant asked.

'Well, I've seen *Beau Geste*, and I like them hats with the curtain on.'

He served for fifteen years in the desert before being discharged and returning home. When he walked through the front door, his wife asked: 'Where have you been?'

'I've been in the Legion.'

'God blimey,' she said. 'What kind of licence have they got there?'

# 8 *Here we go . . . Here we go . . .*

Liverpool is probably the most soccer-mad city in the world. Football takes precedence over politics, religion, even family life. Each year a similar conversation takes place in homes all over Merseyside. The average Scouser turns to his wife and says:

'Now, is there anything you want to say to me before the football season starts?'

To which she usually replies:

'I think you think more of Liverpool than you do of me.'

And the husband remarks:

'I think more of *Everton* than I do of you.'

There is probably no crisis or disaster big enough to take a Scouser's mind off the important question of how his favourite team are faring. One man was seen at the corner table of the pub, crying into his ale. At that moment his pal walked in and asked: 'What's wrong with you, Jim?'

'You might well ask me what's wrong,' he sobbed. 'You might well ask . . .'

'What's wrong, then?'

'Don't ask me. It's all right for you, lad. I came off nights and found the wife had cleared off with the feller from next door . . . The two kids have run away to sea . . . When I got back from the pub this morning the house had burned down . . . And Liverpool lost.'

'Come on, don't upset yourself.'

'Upset meself?' he choked. 'I can't understand it. They were winning at half-time.'

Liverpudlians worship Liverpool and Everton because no two teams have ever enjoyed such a wealth of talent. Each club has one player who can work in any position as well as Maradonna, can hit a ball with either foot, has periferal vision and can head like a dream. The only problem is persuading him to take off his donkey jacket and come out of the crowd.

The wit of Liverpool's Kop crowd is, of course, legendary. At one floodlit game, when the action was sluggish to say the least, the fans were becoming bored. A lone voice shouted: 'Switch them lights off.'

And another, at the back of the Kop, answered: 'D'you mind – I'm reading.'

The Kop is always at its best when it breaks into spontaneous song. Thousands of like-minds burst into the same verse, without prompting. I remember when Gary Sprake of Leeds threw the ball into his own net at Anfield, and the Kop instantly broke into a chorus of 'Careless Hands.'

Liverpudlians can't hold back that lightning wit, even

before the game starts. Crowds were pouring into a Derby game, many without tickets. The streets around Anfield were a sea of Liverpool and Everton supporters – 100,000 fans struggling to fill 70,000 seats.

Police were out in force marshalling the crowds. All around the entrances there were mounted policemen pushing people towards the turnstiles. One Scouser nodded towards them and said to his mate: 'It's stupid, this. You'd think they'd let them horses in first, wouldn't you?'

I was on the Kop watching a Derby game some years ago, when a feller next to me felt the tell-tale signs that he was going to faint. As his eyes rolled up, he turned to his mate and said: 'I'm goin', Joey.'

It was a big crowd that day and his pal looked anxious.

'We'll have to get you out fast,' he said.

There was no clear path to the exits, and no way out onto the field.

'Come on,' he said. 'We'll lift you up. You'll have to go over the top.'

'I did enough of that during the war,' his pal said.

. . . which I didn't think was bad for a bloke who passed out seconds later.

When Liverpool bought Tony Hately, who was celebrated for his high crosses, some critical fans claimed that all he could do was head the ball.

'Waste of money,' one Koppite remarked.

'Na,' said his mate. 'He'll be a complete footballer after the transplant – they're putting a head on both feet.'

At a big game the most unpopular man on the field is the ref. Whatever decision he makes is bound to upset someone. Arthur Ellis, the veteran referee, told me with a twinkle that the secret is to make up your mind, then blame it on someone else. For example:

Liverpool are playing Manchester United at Anfield; it's a sold-out match, and the score is nil-nil. A United forward breaks through and is deliberately tripped in the penalty area. The ref's whistle blows and there is total silence. Whatever he decides, 50,000 people will be waiting to hang him. So he walks straight over to the linesman and says: 'It's crowded here today, isn't it?'

The linesman nods his head, and the ref immediately signals a penalty.

There is nothing to beat the atmosphere of a big game but, with all your ale money in your pocket, you have to be on the lookout for lightfingered thieves. One pickpocket was arrested at Goodison and taken to the city court.

'I think you are a public disgrace, picking the pockets of hardworking dockers,' the magistrate told him. 'Fined fifty pounds.'

'Sir, he's been searched and he only has three pounds on him,' the clerk interrupted.

'Put him back in the crowd until he makes the money up,' the magistrate ordered.

Now, it may not be widely known in the rest of the country, but Merseyside does have a third team. Tranmere are not smiled upon by the gods, but no one could fault them for trying. To be fair, you can't blame the players. In the middle of a match the sound of the scoreboard clock ticking can be very distracting.

When I last went to Tranmere, they were shoving season tickets into your pockets at the turnstiles as you went in. People suffer genuine hardship watching them – you have to walk thirty yards across the terrace to ask for a light. The only consolation is that there is never any

*Would you buy a used car from this man?*

trouble at a game – mainly because it's hard to fight when you are crying.

It was all summed up by a court case in the *Echo*:

'Do you know what an oath is?' the magistrate asked the man in the dock.

'I watch Tranmere, don't I?' he said.

Back in the mists of history Liverpool invented football. The theory was that if Scousers kicked a ball around they would not beat each other's brains out with cudgels. The modern game has become very sophisticated. Basically, there is a big field, surrounded on each side by a shed with one of its walls missing. Into each shed are packed 20,000 people and, when the whistle blows, they start fighting each other.

The game is very selective. The rules only allow twenty-two spectators, who stand in the middle of the field and watch everyone hammering each other.

The only other spectactors permitted are the brass band, but it is clear that they are not happy with what is going on. They spend the whole of half-time marching up and down trying to find a way out.

On the terraces there are three essential items of protection – the oily mac, in case of pigeons; the beer crate – full, of course – for standing on if you are too short; and a pair of big wellies for standing in if you are caught short.

Every couple of years Scousers make the big migration South for the Cup Final. Apart from joining the T.A., it is the only event guaranteed to give married men a weekend away from home. Wives and children line up to wave them off as they climb onto the coach:

' . . . Wave to yer dad. You may never see him again. With a bit of luck.'

Inside the coach the fellers sit by the windows, mouthing, 'I'll give you a ring when I get there, love. God bless.'

And the coach pulls away, but how long can they last before someone cracks?

'Er, we're a bit dry back here, driver. Can you pull up at the first pub you come to?'

And the driver says: 'Hang on, lads. Let me get out of the street.'

The true Scouser would never dream of going to Wembley with a ticket. The tradition is either to go over the wall; flash a Woodbine packet as a Press pass; or line up in formation with mouth-organs to pose as the Irish Guards Band.

About half-past-five, when the game has finished and the pubs are opening, telephones ring simultaneously all over Liverpool:

'Hello, love . . . God, you want to see the fog down here. I'm off to the Salvation Army hostel for the night. If it's not lifted by morning, I'm walking.'

'We didn't see any fog on the telly . . .'

'No, well, it's the special lights they have. They don't pick it up.'

Next day, as darkness fell, three Scousers were driving back from Wembley in a car they had found. They were cruising through the countryside when they passed a huge open field.

'Pull up, Charlie,' one of them said. 'Look at that pig, there. That's bacon for a week – get it in the back.'

A few miles on, the driver picked out a police road-block in his headlights.

'Right lads,' he said. 'They must be looking for the pig. Disguise it, quick.'

In a flash the pig was dressed in a flat cap, oily mac and, for good measure, given a Woodbine. When they pulled up, a policeman shone his torch into the car.

'Okay, you lot,' he said. 'Names.'

DRIVERS OF SLOW VEHICLES
MUST TELEPHONE
BEFORE CROSSING

'Charlie Peterson,' said the driver.

'Jimmy Peterson,' the front passenger said.

'What about you two in the back?' the officer asked.

'Billy Peterson,' said the Scouser and, right on cue, the pig went, 'Oink'.

The roadblock opened and allowed them through. As the car drove away, the policeman turned to his mate and said:

'You know, I've seen some ugly Scousers in my time – but that Oink Peterson . . .'

Half-way home they broke down on the motorway. Luckily, a Rolls pulled over and the driver offered to help.

'It's either the battery or the starter motor,' Charlie said. 'I don't know what's wrong.'

'I've got a tow rope,' the Roller driver said. 'Hook it up, and I'll pull you to the next service station.'

They set off at a steady twenty-five mph until a Porsche flashed past them, playing a tune on its air horns. The Rolls driver could not resist the challenge. Forgetting completely about the tow, he put his foot down and set off in hot pursuit. Soon they were nudging ninety in the fast lane; then a hundred, a hundred-and-fifty . . .

An AA patrolman saw them shoot past him and switched on his radio:

'Harry,' he shouted excitedly to his mate. 'You won't believe what's coming your way. I've never seen anything like it. There's a Porsche and a Roller bumper to bumper doing a hundred-and-fifty. Right behind them there's a little Ford Popular honking his horn like mad, and they won't let him overtake.'

Liverpudlians love any kind of sporting action. Cricket is a little on the slow side for most Scousers, but there was

*Down and out in deepest Elstree*

an historic match played on Merseyside which went completely unreported.

Years ago, when the South African touring team landed in Britain to find themselves banned because of Apartheid, they faced the prospect of going home without a game. On the quayside, before their ship sailed, the manager was chatting to one of the dockers.

'The boys trained hard for the tour,' he complained. 'It's a pity they didn't even get the chance of a knock-around.'

'Listen,' the foreman offered. 'We'll give you a game.'

And within a few minutes he was organizing a team. The foreman could only scrape together ten men, until old Harry walked up with the dock horse. To make it less obvious, they dressed it up in flannels and a sweater and stood it on its hind legs in the slips. The horse caught the first six balls in a blur of hooves.

'Can he bowl?' one of the dockers asked.

'Freddie Trueman rejuvenated,' said old Harry, who cleaned out the stable.

When they stuck a ball in the horse's hoof, it bowled out the whole team.

'Can he bat?' someone asked.

'Another Don Bradman,' Harry promised.

The first ball disappeared half-way to the Isle of Man.

'Run,' the dockers' captain shouted.

'Don't be daft,' said Harry. 'If he could run he'd be at Aintree.'

As Liverpool is the home of the Grand National, Scousers have a keen eye for form, and few can resist the temptation of making a few bob on the horses.

An eighty-two-year-old pensioner drew out his life savings and took the bag of money down to the betting office.

'It's all I've got in the world,' he said. 'And I want it on Red Giant in the three o'clock.'

'Don't back it, grandad,' the manager whispered. 'It's a donkey. You're throwing your money away.'

'Listen, son,' said the old man. 'Just do as you're told. I want £1000 to win on Red Giant in the three o'clock.'

The bookie rang the blower man from his private phone and said:

'Jimmy, there's an old feller here wants to put a grand on Red Giant at 300–1. I can't talk him out of it so, when you do the commentary, crack on that his horse is in with a bit of a chance, will you?'

'Okay, Billy,' he said. 'Leave it to me.'

A few minutes later the tapes were up and the commentary came over the Tannoy:

'They're coming up to the first and Red Giant's tongue is hanging out. They're over the first and approaching the second. Red Giant is puffing and blowing, but he's still there . . .'

At this point there was a break in the transmission. When it resumed a few seconds later he was saying:

'. . . And they're over the last fence. Red Giant is thirty-five lengths clear – and I'm not kiddin', Billy. I'm not kiddin' . . .'

Now, outsiders might be forgiven for thinking that golf is not a sport close to the heart of Liverpudlians. Nothing could be further from the truth. Even the most hardened Koppite will take up the clubs given the opportunity.

The chance came to Jimmy Mack when he won the pools – half a million pounds, and his wife knew exactly what to do with it:

'I wanna get out from round 'ere. I wanna house in Southport with a big yard.'

A month later Jimmy was sitting in his four-acre yard,

soaking his feet in a bucket of water, when his wife said:

'Why don't you take up golf? Get down to that club in Birkdale where they're all posh.'

He went to Jack Sharp's sports shop, asked for a bag of bats, and joined the golf club. On his first outing divots were flying everywhere; the green looked as though a tank training school had been over it. Back at the club house there was uproar at the bar.

'This is absolutely ridiculous,' said the president. 'The man can't even play. He's wrecking the place. Something has to be done about him.'

By this time Jimmy was in the restaurant tucking into a well-earned meat-and-two-veg. A gentleman with a walrus moustache went over to him an announced: 'I'm Colonel Smythe, I'm in charge of the greens here.'

'I wanna see you, pal,' said Jimmy. 'These sprouts are rubbish . . .'

# 9 *School for Scouse*

Whatever their official education, Scousers enrol early at the university of life. Even toddlers are more advanced today than their parents ever were. Take this conversation I overheard in Liverpool:

> LITTLE BOY: 'How old are you?'
> PAL: 'Dunno but I think I'm six.'
> LITTLE BOY: 'Do women worry you?'
> PAL: 'No.'
> LITTLE BOY: 'Well, you're about four.'

It always strikes me as odd in an overpopulated world, that people place the blame on sexual ignorance. If we had a little more ignorance there might be fewer of us. The trouble is that kids want to know about life too early.

It can be a terrible problem when they march home from school and ask: 'Hey dad, where did I come from?'

Father begins by stuttering: 'Well, er, son . . .' and takes him into the front room and shuts the door. After two hours of stumbling through the birds and bees, dad is sweating bullets. He has demolished forty cigarettes and he is gasping for a pint because his throat has dried up. Exhausted, he asks:

'Why did you want to know where you come from?'

'Dunno,' says the boy. 'It's just that the lad next to me in school said he came from Birmingham.'

When I was young everything worked by the 'askyou' method:

'Where do I come from, dad?'

'Ask your mother.'

'Where do I come from mum?'

'Ask your teacher.'

'Where do I come from, Miss?'

'Well, it's all very strange and wonderful. It's rather like a little miracle.'

'It must be, because me mum and dad don't know, and I'm here.'

Children have not changed since I was teaching. In Liverpool they still go around in clothes too big for them. Scouse mums buy everything two sizes too large so that kids can grow into them.

The highlight of every Monday morning was gathering in the sick notes. One, I recall, read:

Dear Sir,

Our Daryl couldn't come today because he hasn't been. I'll give him something to make him go and, as soon as he's been, he'll come.

Mrs Reilly.

I taught at both the Bootle junior and senior schools which I had attended as a boy. They were old buildings with all the drawbacks associated with them. Rats were the least of our problems – we got rid of them by putting down school dinners.

The head of the Catholic secondary was one of the old school. On the first day he took me aside and gave me two pieces of advice. The first was:

'Never trust a nun, son. You won't know your throat's been cut till your head starts nodding.'

He followed this with:

'You'll find out that teaching these kids is like shovelling smoke with a billiard cue.'

Some of the pupils, I found, could hardly write their own name but, for their age, had mathematical minds bordering on genius. They could calculate a yankee bet, with all the odds and permutations, faster than any adult. And, of course, they always had a quick answer for everything:

'If any of you go on to art school,' one teacher said, 'you may have to paint portraits in the nude.'

'I'd have to leave me socks on, sir,' said one lad. 'I'd have nowhere to put me brushes.'

Scouse parents have to be sharp, because they know that their children can drag them into trouble when they least expect it. Every year they come home from holiday through the green channel to be stopped by the customs officer:

'Anything to declare, sir? Perfume, cameras, cigarettes?'

'No. Nothing at all.'

And the kids tug at their father's sleeve and say:

'He was close, though, wasn't he, dad?'

Some of them, in street terms, are too smart for school.

One of my pupils complained to his parents: 'I can't read, I can't write and they won't let me talk.'

Scousers are very secretive. When I was earning seven pounds a week as a teacher, kids were leaving school to earn thirty pounds a week screwing on headlamps at Ford's. If anyone asked what they did for a living, they would always say, 'Not a lot,' or 'as little as possible.'

In the same way, you can dial any number in Liverpool and never get a straight answer.

'Hello, is Tony in?'

'Tony who?'

Liverpudlian policy is that the rest of the world should operate on a strictly need-to-know basis.

I almost lost my job taking forty-eight kids on an educational trip to London. It was a rough school, and they had no uniforms. The day before we left I insisted that they all had to wear one item of the same colour, so that I could keep an eye on them.

Next morning, I tried to ignore the fact that they had all turned up in grey to blend with the crowd. After touring the Tower of London and the British Museum, I allowed them to do some shopping, with firm orders to be back at Euston at a certain time. At the station I took no chances and counted them in. There were forty-six.

'Where's the other two?' I asked.

'They won't be long, sir,' everybody chorused.

I warned them that if they were not back in five minutes we would all miss the train. A few lads immediately disappeared and came back with them. I counted the heads again, and there were forty-eight.

At Lime Street station the head was waiting. The first thing he did was insist that they all turned out their

*'Ello, 'ello, 'ello*

pockets. Shoplifted souvenirs of London fell onto the platform. Then he turned to me and asked for the register. I told him that I hadn't checked the names, but had counted heads, and everyone was present and correct.

The old headmaster knew better. When he called everyone's names on the list, only forty-six answered. Hiding at the back of the group we found two Cockney kids who had been hijacked from Euston to make up the numbers. And somewhere in London two young Scousers were half-way through a very long pub crawl.

My subjects were maths and music – sums and drums, the kids called them. Music teaching was thrust upon me when the regular teacher cracked under the strain and ran away from school.

Choosing careers at the end of the school year was always a problem. One September a mother brought back her son, who had left in July.

'Look at the state of him,' she complained to the head. 'The hair on that, now. And the boots. You wouldn't recognize him. Can't get a job, can yer?'

'Er, no mam. There's nothin' down for me. I wanted to be a brain surgeon, but they've only got brickies' jobs.'

'You passed exams, though, didn't you?' she said.

'Oh, yeah. I got exams, like.'

'What exams has he passed?' the headmaster asked.

'Art and religion,' the mother said.

'Well, get him to bang in for a job painting holy pictures.'

Religion was taught extensively, but it was always doubtful whether the message sank in.

'What did yer get learned today?' another mother asked her son when he came home from school.

'We got learned all kinds. They was learnin' us about

Moses. You know, getting the Israelites out of Egypt. It was a gear story.'

'Why, what happened?'

'Well, Moses was havin' a pipe round Egypt, and he said to his mate: "It looks a bit barley to me, Jim. I think we ought to bale out." So they went round all the alehouses and said: "Get yer tackle on yer backs – we're leggin' it." They shot out of Eygpt together, more like a chara than anything.

'Across the desert, the Pharoah's after them. Moses had a bit of a start on them, like. And, er, they got to the Red Sea. And Moses said: "Hang on, a bit of a problem's come up." So a feller asked him: "What are you going to do, Mose?" He said: "Just button that, lad, till I'm ready. Now, this is what we're goin' to do. For a start we'll throw a bridge across this river. We'll get everybody over the water, then we'll turn round and wellie them."

'So they got across and threw all their tanks and guns and rockets at the Pharaoh's army and blew 'em to bits.'

'Is that the way they teached it you in school?' his mother asked.

'No. But the way they told it in school, mam, you'd never believe it.'

Stories used to circulate in school about Liverpool's own unofficial history, as far back as the Romans. When Britain was conquered, in 55 BC, one tale ran, Liverpool was the last region to hold out. Twenty-five thousand legionnaires closed in on the King of Liverpool's cave. They surrounded it in gleaming armour, until the king finally put down his copy of the *Echo* and walked to the entrance in his flat cap.

'Alright, Julius,' he called. 'Send in your hardest man.'

A twenty-stone legionnaire, loaded with armour, strode towards the cave. All the Roman army could hear

*On the Roadshow*

inside was a butt-butt, stomp-stomp, wellie-wellie sound. Then the king came out again, and said:

'Okay, Julius, send in your next five hardest men.'

The five charged in on horseback, and the same sounds were heard again. The King of Liverpool emerged without a scratch.

'I'll give you one last chance, Julius,' he shouted. 'Send in twenty-five men, all at once, in chariots.'

There was a thunder of hooves as they rode into the cave. Minutes later, one of them staggered out, battered and bleeding.

'Julius,' he gasped. 'Don't send any more. It's a trap. There's two of them in there.'

# 10 *Christmas Crackers*

It may not have the lights of Regent Street, but there is one sure way to tell that it is Christmas in Liverpool – the Easter eggs are on sale in Woolies window. Families are reunited, and those with student lodgers have the house to themselves again.

'Bye, son. He's a nice lad, Mary. Taking medicine at the university.'

'Is it doing him any good?'

On Christmas Eve the men of the house are always down at the pub. You can spot them when you walk in – each one has sixteen pints of bitter on a tray, and a couple of pints wedged under each arm for good measure. And they are saying:

'. . . As long as the kids are enjoying themselves, that's the main thing.'

The pub is also an ideal place to buy any last-minute presents which may have been overlooked:

'Wanna buy a watch?'

'Let's have a look at it.'

'Ssh. The feller next to you's wearin' it.'

Christmas, of course, means panto time – that great annual tradition which takes me back to the time when I was appearing in Aladdin at the Liverpool Empire. Two little boys were standing outside looking at the poster:

'How much is it?' one asked.

'Two pound fifty in the stalls,' his mate said.

'What a fiddle,' said the lad. 'They charge all that money and treat you like horses.'

The whole family gets together for Christmas dinner, and they are all having a great time, until they tuck into the turkey:

'Dad,' says the youngest. 'This turkey doesn't half taste funny. And has anyone seen Harry, my rabbit?'

Not a cough.

'I'm just saying, dad. This turkey tastes funny, And has anyone seen Harry?'

No one spoke.

'Dad, we're not eating Harry, are we?'

'No, son. We're eatin' a duck. And it was a naughty duck. It ate Harry.'

On Christmas night everyone converges on the pub. The whole place is swinging and, right in the middle, there is always one woman, crying. She sobs all night, and her husband completely ignores her:

'. . . Shine On . . . Shine On Harvest Moon . . . all sway the one way now . . . come on . . .'

It is not until closing time that he notices her crying, and asks what is the matter:

*Fun with the Princess Royal*

'Somebody should have been with our Jimmy,' she sobs.

'But our Jimmy's in America.'

'I don't care. Somebody should have been with him at Christmas.'

'America's three thousand miles away.'

'He's on his own there. Somebody should have been with him.'

'But Jimmy's thirty-seven.'

'He should never have gone on his own.'

'All right,' says the husband, who can't take any more. 'I'm going. Now. To America.'

His mate pulls him back by the sleeve and says: 'You can't go now, the buses have stopped. How are you gonna get there?'

'I'm gonna row,' says the husband.

The entire pub empties and everyone goes down to the riverside, where there is a little dinghy and a pair of oars. Ten minutes later, the husband is loaded up for the transatlantic voyage – five crates of Guinness and five-hundred Woodies. He jumps in and stikes out for the New World as the women wish him well:

'God bless you, Charlie . . .'

'Safe home, son . . .'

'God go with you, lad . . .'

They kept the pub open until twelve o'clock as a goodbye-to-Charlie night. At about ten to twelve, one of Charlie's mates turned to the landlord, and asked:

'Did you, er, take the towrope off that boat?'

'No,' the landlord said.

'Well, he's still tied up to the quay, then.'

They went down to dock again and, in the darkness,

*Please Sir – me in my teaching days*

they could still hear the oars swishing rhythmically. One of them shouted: 'Charlie . . .'

And a voice came back: 'God blimey – no one knows me in America.'